AROUND THE WORLD BY CRUISE SHIP

AROUND THE WORLD BY CRUISE SHIP

People, Places, Politics

Elizabeth G. Reininga

Copyright © 2000 by Elizabeth G. Reininga.

Library of Congress Number: 00-192294
ISBN #: Hardcover 0-7388-3991-4
Softcover 0-7388-3992-2

All rights reserved. No part of this book may be reproduced or transmitted in any form or by any means, electronic or mechanical, including photocopying, recording, or by any information storage and retrieval system, without permission in writing from the copyright owner.

Cover Photo: Antarctica on a rare sunny day from the aft deck of the Rotterdam, January 28, 2000.

This book was printed in the United States of America.

To order additional copies of this book, contact:
Xlibris Corporation
1-888-7-XLIBRIS
www.Xlibris.com
Orders@Xlibris.com

CONTENTS

MILLENIUM IN THE CARIBBEAN	15
THE WORLD CRUISE BEGINS— FT. LAUDERDALE	19
GRAND CAYMAN	21
PANAMA CANAL	22
ECUADOR—MANTA	25
PERU—CALLAO	27
PERU—GENERAL SAN MARTIN	29
CHILE—ARICA	32
CHILE—COQUIMBO	34
CHILE—VALPARAISO	37
CHILE—PUERTO MONTT	39
CHILE—PUNTA ARENAS	41
ARGENTINA—USHUAIA	44
ARGENTINA—CAPE HORN	46
ANTARCTICA	47
ARGENTINA—BUENOS AIRES	55
TRISTAN DA CUNHA	57
SOUTH AFRICA—CAPETOWN	59
SOUTH AFRICA—DURBAN	62
MADAGASCAR—NOSY BÉ	66
TANZANIA—ZANZIBAR	69
KENYA—MOMBASA	73
SEYCHELLES—VICTORIA	77
SEYCHELLES—PRASLIN	78
MALDIVES—MALÉ	80
INDIA—COCHIN	83
INDIA—MADRAS	85

THAILAND—PHUKET 95
SINGAPORE 98
VIETNAM—VUNG TAU 100
CHINA—HONG KONG 102
CHINA—SHANGHAI 108
CHINA—XINGANG 111
CHINA—DALIAN 116
SOUTH KOREA—CHEJU CITY 119
JAPAN—NAGASAKI 121
JAPAN—KAGOSHIMA 123
JAPAN—OSAKA 126
JAPAN—TOKYO 128
MIDWAY ISLAND 132
UNITED STATES—HONOLULU, HAWAII 135
UNITED STATES—
    KAILUA-KONA 140
UNITED STATES—
    LOS ANGELES 144
MEXICO—CABO SAN LUCAS 146
MEXICO—ACAPULCO 147
MEXICO—SANTA CRUZ-HUATULCO 148
COSTA RICA—PUERTO CALDERA 150
PANAMA CANAL—AGAIN 152
CURACAO—WILLEMSTAD 153
UNITED STATES—FT. LAUDERDALE 154

WORLD CRUISE RECIPES 157

ORDER FORM 169

For this planet we call earth,
Its times and its tides
Its sunsets and seasons,
Its fruitfulness and fragility,
We give thanks.

> Adapted from
> O. Eugene Pickett

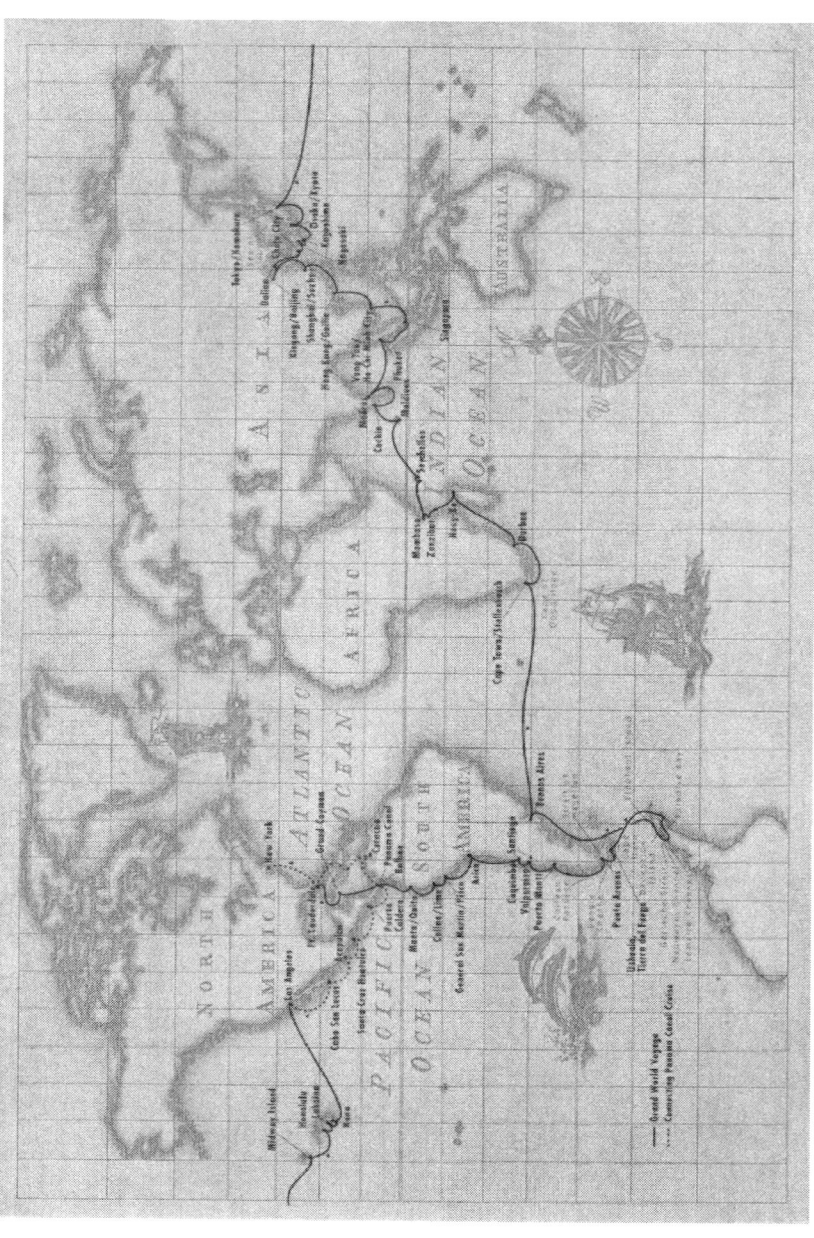

To the oceans of the world,
and to the men who sail upon them—
Captains Conrad Menke, Jacob Dijk and Pieter Bos,
of Holland America Line.

This narrative has been aided and encouraged by a number of friends. My appreciation is owed to Lynn and Chuck Anderson, Margaret Binnendyk, Joann and Bill Blackburn, Dr. Harm J. de Blij, Frances Dew, Natalie Hannum, Anne Johnson, Joanne Schweik and Betty Thompson. You know I am grateful.

Most of all, my husband, Pete, supports, encourages and participates in every adventure. We have gone many happy miles together.

The delightful urge to chuck our responsibilities and go to the ends of the earth comes over us often these days. We respect and enjoy this phase of life. In the past twelve years, we have taken two sixty-day cruises—one around the Orient and another around South America, and the 1996 World Cruise, plus more than a dozen one week and ten-day cruises. At times, various friends join us and many have become repeat travelers. We re-establish friendships with folks we have known from other voyages as soon as we walk on board, so every ship feels like home.

Travel by ship is our choice because we love being able to unpack our clothes and stay in a clean environment. Holland America Line satisfies our needs, is a price we can afford and the Dutch are reliable sailors. We sometimes need the emergency services of the ship. Holland America engineers have repaired Pete's leg brace when he needs help en route. That guttural voice over the loudspeaker every day inspires trust. The attention of the line to details gives us confidence.

Our travel agent is Cruise Specialists of Seattle. Their office is a long way from either of the places where we live, in western New York, and in Florida. However, distance presents no obstacles. The agency is generous, with gifts, shore excursions and cocktail parties on World Cruises and with a bottle of wine and shipboard credit on shorter ones. Our account agent anticipates our requirements better than we do. It is comforting to know that she will book our preferences for dinner on the ship and seats on the airplane, without having to be told each time.

MILLENIUM IN THE CARIBBEAN

DECEMBER 30, 1999 We set sail from Ft. Lauderdale with our twin sons, Dan and David, their wives, Wendy and Kathy, and four of their six children on the ms Rotterdam, flagship of the Holland America Line, for a one week Millennium cruise. We are stacked like cordwood in three adjoining cabins on Main Deck. Pete and I room with nine-year-old Mark. Kathy and David have their eight-year-old son, Derek, in with them. The third cabin houses Wendy, Dan, Elizabeth and seven-year-old Parker. We are on board together because we are determined to create something memorable for the start of this very special year. Pat and Julian McQuiston, friends from Fredonia, are also on board with us. They are good sports, stiff-upper-lip sorts, who add sophistication to the family group.

December 31, 1999 is the last day of the old century. The ship is in the Bahamas for the day and sails in the early afternoon. As evening approaches, excitement builds. Televised celebrations on CNN gather momentum as the New Year arrives around the world. Everyone dresses formally for dinner. The children eat at six and the rest of us at 8:15. Our grandsons look ill at ease in their suits, white shirts and ties but they are awestruck enough to behave. Elizabeth has won part of her battle for the kind of dress she wants. At eleven years of age, she is dressed in black with a glittery jacket. Wendy has a new seafoam green dress and Kathy wears a sparkly black top and long skirt. The three Reininga men are dignified in their black tie outfits.

Dinner is festive, with white cloth chair covers and tablecloths, favors on the table and a special menu: filet mignon, lobster and lamb are the entrees, or all three if we choose. Dessert is chocolate mousse in delicate tulip-shape cups, with a chocolate sign printed in edible gold for both the Rotterdam and the Millennium.

Excitement builds, especially among our young grandchildren. As midnight approaches, everyone congregates up on Lido deck, around the swimming pool. The band plays and colorful confetti roars in a great cloud from compressed air cannons, getting in our hair and piling up 4" deep on the deck. Horns and noisemakers squeal. The new millennium is announced by loudspeaker. As happens every New Year's Eve, Pete and I stand thigh to thigh, looking into each other's eyes, waiting for the right moment to say "Happy New Year" and kiss. The mighty horn of the Rotterdam bellows its news that the year's four digits have changed. The band plays Auld Lang Syne. Tightly pressed passengers sway with the music. There are more than fourteen hundred of us sharing the moment, happy to be alive. We are experiencing nine finales in one split second—the end of the second, minute, hour, day, month, year, decade, century and millennium. In spite of all the media predictions of chaos, terrorism and disruptions around the world, we are here and functioning. The ship sails calmly into the new era.

Holland America gives each passenger a gift, a special Waterford champagne glass to commemorate the Millennium. The toast that comes with it quotes Alfred, Lord Tennyson, "Ring out the thousand years of war. Ring in the thousand years of peace." We pray for that.

* * * * *

Mark is a wonderful cabin mate, up high in the air in his overhead bunk. He is quiet and thoughtful, tiptoeing in to get what he needs if we are asleep. He keeps us up until midnight almost every night but he willingly takes a nap in the daytime. He has his normal nine year old patterns—never picks up his clothes, forgets to flush, loses his watch and wallet frequently, but his easy attitude toward life is a joy to us both. Wendy and Dan have Elizabeth on the couch in their cabin and Parker is like a little cloud on a bunk overhead. He is too young to quite keep up with the older children and most days he's in a state of unhappy disagreement with everything. He frustrates his parents at every turn.

Elizabeth clings to her Mother's company. The two of them share lots of girl secrets. She is just beginning to wear lipstick and there are two or three blemishes on her chin that need lots of attention from the makeup salesgirl. Her skin is naturally clear and beautiful so the clerk is challenged to find ways to sell her products.

Derek, in the center cabin with Kathy and David, can pick up a boy cousin on either side when he's ready for fun. He's five feet tall at age eight, a big big boy on his way up. David and Derek went shopping for a suit for the formal nights on board. I didn't know you could spend $325 on a suit for a child, but we now accept that he qualifies as a small full-size man.

We gave everyone this Millennium trip so we can share the important New Year holiday. When we realized that the cruise line doubled their prices for the holiday season and then doubled them again for this particular trip, we nearly backed out. We mentioned the possibility of canceling, but the children replied to our probing by saying they were counting on it. So we are here on board, to the tune of $400 per person, per day. The ship is full.

The Bahamas, the Virgin Islands and the Dominican Republic are all interesting ports, but the main attraction is being together. I recall lying in bed when I was about Elizabeth's age, dreaming of living to the year 2000 and thinking how very old I would be, if I made it. Now sixty-something doesn't seem quite so old.

One noon David, Kathy, Pete and I have lunch with Kathy's parents' friends, Caroline and Charles. Caroline is little and peppy and feeling well. They are traveling with a large group of friends from Dallas. She later tells Kathy's Dad, Moe, and her mother, Sylvia, that she wishes she had signed on with them for the whole

World Cruise. Caroline leaves Sylvia a bag of cruise clothes when she gets off.

The children really enjoy Holland America's private island, Half Moon Cay. The beach and water sports are aimed at the younger passengers. The whole family basks in the sun, plays in the water and competes in the games.

* * * * *

Our week together flies by. One of the advantages of ship travel is that young children can be free on the ship to get around by themselves. It is fun to see them speak to people they don't know with confidence. In this precarious world of the 21st century, that is a rare event.

We are staying on board, after the week with the family, for the ninety-six-day World Cruise to follow. The way we decided to take "the World" was almost an afterthought. I asked Pete if we could have a little more ship time after the family went home. He said, "O K," and asked where it went. I said it didn't matter where it went, the question to ask was when did it get back. He said, "O K, when does it get back?" I replied, "The eleventh of April in Los Angeles." His reply was, "Oh, another World Cruise. I guess we could do that." Then Moe called one day and announced that they had signed on for the whole trip too. It will be fun to see things through their eyes.

Before they go, twin sons with strong arms help us move from Main deck to our upstairs Verandah mini-suite. Our sons make short work of any project. We are ambivalent about seeing them go—sorry to have an end to the fun we have had together, glad for a chance for real rest and relaxation after the constant activity. The younger generations depart in a flurry of suitcases, souvenirs and hugs.

THE WORLD CRUISE BEGINS—
FT. LAUDERDALE

JANUARY 6TH Kathy's parents, Sylvia and Moe Craddock are already in Ft. Lauderdale. We have shared lots of excitement in the past few months at the prospect of traveling together for ninety-six days. Numerous phone calls have occurred as we've made plans for the shore excursions we will take together.

The Craddocks came from Dallas yesterday and last night they went to the Cruise Specialists' farewell party. Our travel agency always provides a lovely cocktail and dinner party as a send-off for their World Cruise clients. Gifts for the trip were distributed—practical navy blue fleece vests and good looking safari hats. We are sorry to have missed the send-off but are looking forward to everyone's arrival. We have traveled before with two dozen people who are coming on board.

Anne Johnson, our cruise consultant and two other gals from Seattle are on the ship today. We run into them in the halls, pushing a heavy cart, loaded with cartons of expandable paper penguins. They tape one on each client's door until they are visible on every hall. The penguins generate lots of curiosity from other passengers.

Rotterdam sails at 5 PM amid "Bon Voyages" and cheers from the dock. It is a thrill when the ship begins to move, for we know we'll be on board for more than three months. The cabin is chaotic, with suitcases stacked everywhere. Fortunately the first night is casual. We shower and dress for dinner. We will eat at table M with Lynn and Chuck Anderson, Washingtonians we have known from past trips. Their friends, Gene and Peggy Masica, Peggy Masica's sister-in-law, Beth Ingram, and her friend, Jackie Coen, from Kansas City, and the Craddocks round out the table for ten.

Our waiter is Suke, a tall good looking Indonesian of twenty-four, who will serve our dinners for the whole trip. He and his helpers are eager to please in any way they can.

After dinner, the dance troupe presents a show called "Calendar Girl," the same performance we saw on New Year's Eve. The lush stage production involves elaborate costumes for each major season of the year. We enjoy the nightly entertainment—a little glimpse of Hollywood or Las Vegas every night.

Staff officers for Holland America Line for this cruise include Captain Jacob Dijk, First Officer Arjen van der Loo, Chief Engineer Gerard Hijmans, and Hotel Manager, Fekko Ebbens. They and their staff of 500 will keep us safe, comfortable and functioning—a big responsibility.

We are in our first mini-suite this trip, complete with its own private balcony. The cabin is spacious, with a VCR and refrigerator and lots of drawers. At the moment the air conditioning isn't working well. Someone will have to look into that for us.

GRAND CAYMAN

JANUARY 8TH At our first port I go into town to A. H. Riise to buy liquor for the cabin parties we expect to give. Our thought is that we will have drinks in the cabin some nights and entertain our friends. I really stock up, including a big bottle of Amaretto for those luxurious nights on the balcony when we leave port and can watch the lights fade away as the ship sails.

We work at unpacking. Formal dress evenings begin right away. We expect to have about thirty-three of them on a trip this long. Our late dinner hour, 8:15, makes for some changes in our day.

Now that we are on board and the trip has begun, a great wave of relaxation sets in. On a long cruise, we take our time about getting adjusted to the new schedule. One of the first nights on board the Cruise staff is introduced. Talkative Gary Walker is Cruise Director. One of the cute members of his staff is Emily O'Brien from Colorado. She is fair and pretty and looks like the girl next door. Shane and Mark are young and optimistic looking. The Cruise Staff runs the sports activities and hosts Bingo. Hostess Holly Fraser, a stunning blonde, from Oregon is in charge of Chat Time and supervises other activities. All of them are attentive to our requests and helpful with problems.

PANAMA CANAL

JANUARY 10TH I feel like I am breathing marshmallows. The air is thick. At 6:30 AM sky and sea are complimentary shades of dark and light grey and the humidity is intense. Inhaling is sniffing in moisture, perhaps good for the face, like a sauna. This humid atmosphere makes the Canal possible: rain falls, fills Gatun lake, feeds the canal locks and flows to the oceans. The Canal raises ships up eighty-five feet, carries them across the Continental Divide, down eighty-five feet and out to sea. One transit uses 50 million gallons of fresh water. The cost of the day to the Rotterdam is nearly eighty thousand dollars but it saves us eight thousand miles circling South America. Crossing the canal will take all day and there will be a lot to watch during the transit.

In my mind this is the real departure from home. The Caribbean has beautiful islands and wonderful music but it is still more like than unlike the United States. After today's crossing, the Canal will spit us out into waters filled with Spanish speaking people, exotic cultures and cocaine smugglers.

As we approach the Canal, I daydream about how it must have been nearly a hundred years ago. Those were Gold Rush Days—and the whole world wanted to be part of the boom. I have a relative, William Gerow, who was an engineer during the construction. He was in his forties and boss of a construction gang of Dominicans or Haitians. During his stay in the land of snakes, yellow fever and constant rain, he found life easier than he did on his return home. When he went back to Smithfield, Ontario, he learned that his wife, Hattie, had run off with an Italian musician from New York City. He followed them to New York to get her back and was never heard from again. Contemporaries thought he was murdered. I wonder if any construction records from those days still exist.

Our Canal crossing is shared with Moe and Sylvia, Chuck and Lynn, Frank Clyne, and the Wolf, Wolff, Rife and Ramery group we remember from other cruises. They arrive around ten AM for Bloody Marys and the view from our balcony as we sail through the historic cuts. We take lots of photos and have our first real chance to visit. Lunch intervenes and then some of our friends return after Lake Gatun for the second set of locks. The balcony stateroom has been a real asset today. We've enjoyed easy access to the outside.

Commentary provided by the Canal goes on all day long. Our heads are bursting with facts by late afternoon. Panama has just taken over the ownership and operation of the canal. On this, their sixth day, everything runs smoothly.

* * * * *

Sylvia and Moe seem bewildered but willing as they explore the shipboard activities. Their first attraction is to the gym and the treadmills. They begin daily participation in Sit and Be Fit, Stretch and Relax and Tai Chi. They work out so much they need naps during the day. A stamp is given for each physical improvement class they take and their goal is to earn enough stamps to get white waffle weave bathrobes by the end of the trip.

At Table M every night the talk is quiet, neighbor to neighbor. As the first week passes, the conversations begin to fly back and forth across the table. Pete is slowly easing into joke telling. Beth and Jackie from Kansas City decorate the table with their impeccable clothes and enthusiasm. The Masicas are experienced cruisers. Gene is a retired submarine commander. His wife, Peggy, has a great sense of humor. Her favorite food is beef, with no gravy.

Chuck Anderson has a perpetual twinkle in his eyes. Lynn Anderson is his right hand woman. Chuck and Pete had polio about the same time, fifty years ago, and they have to cope with varying degrees of difficulty, but both have a "can-do" attitude. Moe and Sylvia complete the circle. They wish they were at early sitting. Getting up from the dinner table at ten at night is late for their early waking exercise habits.

At a table by himself near us is a single man. He has a lean face and a quiet manner. After the first week or two passes, we try to find out something about him. His name is Larry. The dance instructor says he is a nice man who has had a bout with cancer and is trying to complete a whole World Cruise. Beth tries to make eye contact with him and smiles, but he is skillful at avoiding her eyes. Of course, she is intimidatingly beautiful. That may have something to do with it. Moe has more luck than Beth and soon he and Larry are talking about their new digital cameras and exchanging pictures.

The food is wonderful. Suke pays strict attention to our requests and makes a big show of bringing the dessert tray for us to admire every night. He tells us the fattening desserts are wonderful and the low calorie suggestions are not what we would enjoy.

ECUADOR—MANTA

JANUARY 12TH The soft grey light of pre-dawn calls me to the railing outside. We are gently sliding into an odd-smelling port that has few lights. The smells on the air speak of unknown spices, tar, oil, fish. Small fishing boats are crossing the harbor. A male voice from the grey sea calls "Hola, Amigo!" with a wave of his hand, as his boat scurries behind our stern.

The mighty Rotterdam looks out of place as she comes to shore, like a large animal that needs help. Her rightful place is at sea, in command of her world. Now she resigns herself to being attached to the pier for twelve hours, until she can go free again.

We tie up where four large fishing boats are docked. Their cranes for lifting the huge fishing nets have booms thirty feet long with giant pulleys at the tops of the arms. Black nets piled on the stern decks of each boat take up as much space as a small house.

Our shore excursion takes us to the Indian market. On the way we hear from the guide about the economic crisis gripping Equador. The government has just announced that the currency of the country will in two months be pegged to the American dollar. With nearly twenty per cent of the population out of work, conditions have been confusing for the last year and a half. The guide says that if you don't work, you don't eat. If you don't eat, you die. We see this vividly in hordes of children with their mothers, begging at every tourist stop.

At the Indian Market children waggle woven things under our noses as we try to go inside. When I come back out to the bus, I look at all these children, most the age of our grandchildren. One skinny ten-year-old boy with stringy black hair and a small pointed face pleadingly holds a woven piggy bank up to me. He waves two fingers to say it costs two dollars. Such a little bit of money for a hand-woven toy. I nod and meet him at the door of the bus to hand over my two dollars. I make it known, with the help of the driver, that I want another one just like it. He disappears and comes back in a few minutes with the second bank.

The bus waits in the heat of the street for the rest of the passengers to return. Suddenly I notice the boy jumping up so he can see over the heads of the crowd outside the bus window. He is smaller than most of the kids in the crowd and he repeatedly jumps to see over them. When he realizes I see him, he smiles and voices "Thank you." You wonder about the children of the world: where they sleep, how they eat, who takes care of them, and how much difference four dollars can make in their lives.

There is lots of activity on the dock when we return. Soldiers have discovered seven thousand pounds of heroin in the ship tied to the dock in front of us. Enforcement officers are everywhere. Two helicopters hover in the sky. The ship is locked down and no-one can go near her. Ecuador shares a common border with Columbia. It is difficult for this country to police the jungle border where drugs are smuggled through from the north. This is a reminder of the drug trade that is destroying our cities back home.

PERU—CALLAO

JANUARY 14TH We first visited Peru ten years ago on a Grand Voyage around South America. It was one of my favorite stops. What an exotic country. Today the air is green and dripping with the reek of fish. I feel as if taking in a deep lung-full might line my chest with living seaweed. What a stink! The air is motionless and thick; there is no fresh air to be had.

Callao is the port for Lima. We've already seen the pre-Columbian gold, the weaving and the pillboxes on the street corners where gun emplacements are located in the capital city. Our shore excursion goes through Callao to another Indian market. We happily shop in the developing countries because goods that are grown, processed and sold locally are duty free at United States Customs.

Whenever we are out in the public spaces on foot, we prepare as if going into battle. Left in the cabin are diamond rings and good watches. We carry wallet and purse in front, close to the body, sometimes under a jacket. Only one credit card goes on shore, only small amounts of cash and we never ever carry passports with us. We try not to flaunt our possessions, but it is hard to be inconspicuous when you wear big white gym shoes, bright clothes, a red jacket and have blonde hair. Pete and I travel in non-English speaking ports on ship's Shore Excursions: we hope for safety in numbers and a reliable English-speaking escort. We could go ashore on our own, but we will reduce the amount of territory we cover and our understanding of the country. It is an odd fact that Christian countries have much more street crime than there is in the Muslim world. I wonder what that says about our moral code?

The new check-off, check-on system at the gangplank slows our exit from the ship. Some of the really elderly passengers are confused by the machine that scans our cards as we leave and again when we return. It certainly is better than the old system where no-one knew who had gone ashore and who had not. With this new method, there is just one ID card that works for every purpose, including opening the door to our cabin.

The Lido on a HAL ship is a large brightly lit cafeteria, self-service, with chefs behind the counter dispensing daily specials. For passengers who go there often, it is a place where they get as many servings of one food as they want, heaped on a plate to the outer rim. Some people carry away six eggs or a pound of bacon at a time. Others eat huge quantities of fresh fruit. There is more variety in the fruit served up there than there is in the dining room. You can make your own salads in the Lido. But the most popular place of all is the ice cream and dessert section. A range of elegant desserts is displayed, including all the special baked items from the previous day's High Tea or Dessert Extravaganza. Cholesterol clogs the arteries from simply walking past the counter.

The Rotterdam's famous bread pudding with vanilla sauce is served there. Six varieties of ice cream and frozen yogurt with six choices of sprinkles and four ice cream sauces, four bottles of liquors and whipped cream can be mixed and matched to each taste. We head straight for the hot dog and hamburger bar when we return from a Shore Excursion.

The Lido is also a blessing for those passengers who dance until the wee hours at ship's party evenings. The midnight buffet is a last chance for them to eat before bedtime. If they want to sleep late in the morning, breakfast is available until ten.

PERU—GENERAL SAN MARTIN

JANUARY 15TH I have found the wandering sands of the Sahara in the Paracas peninsula of Peru. Here rain comes in less than two millimeter annual showers, creating the arid atmosphere of the Atacama Desert, reputed to be the driest place on earth. The aqua blue of the sea and the paler clear blue of the sky set off the tans, greys, reds, yellows and black of endless sand dunes. Dusty slopes define the landscape, reaching against the sky, shifting with the daily afternoon wind.

Pete and the Craddocks are all excited about their scheduled flight over the Nasca Lines this morning. They fly back into the Andes where they see pictures drawn on the arid desert by a civilization that lived 1500 years ago. It is a memorable morning for them viewing the huge angular figures scratched into the desert.

I take a bus to the Paracas museum. Kika, our guide, offers a tapestry of facts to supplement very few exhibits. Since woven Paracas mantles are world famous, I had hoped to see one here, but the museum is small and primitive and there are none. Such beautiful textiles need security and climate control equipment. Here where they were woven, buried as wrappings for mummies and then dug out of the sand a thousand years later, there are none. I am disappointed in the facility but the bus ride is fascinating, through miles of desert and deserted hills.

We climb into the foothills of the Andes to visit Tambo Colorado, an ancient Inca warehouse complex, with a series of brown stone cubicles that were housing for the workers. A perpetual breeze funnels up the valley from the sea, making the heat bearable. Setting, colors and wind suggest what this place might have been hundreds of years ago. Ruins colored red like the desert are ranged along the side of the hill.

We climb through various storage chambers and living spaces surrounding the central square. The atmosphere whispers of people who lived here before white men came. I hear children racing around the high stone walls.

It must have been difficult to raise crops in this valley. Positioned at the head of the valley, halfway up the slope, Tambo Colorado has a long perspective. I leave reluctantly, wishing there were more time and a chance to be alone among the stones.

Our third stop is Hacienda San José', a working farm in operation since the 1600s. The Cincha river ranch grows citrus, grapes, asparagus and avocados and is also a tourist hotel. Tables are arranged on a long shady porch overlooking the back courtyard. We begin with deep fried yucca strips and mustard sauce, with the locally famous drink, Pisco Sours—a margarita-like cocktail made of brandy, lemon juice, sugar syrup and egg white. Lunch is a Creole buffet, meaning we can expect food prepared to reflect the European traditions combined with Spanish seasonings. Several chicken dishes, asparagus, beans, tamales, chili, rice and fried dough ovals with vanilla syrup for dessert feed us abundantly. The young woman who owns the ranch joins us for lunch, in her blue jeans and with newly washed hair. She speaks excellent English.

The courtyard of the house is colorful. Acacia trees throw their flame-orange blooms over walls and trellises. A swimming pool is surrounded by cascades of pink and yellow bougainvillea.

After lunch I wander through the silence of the hacienda with its high ceilinged rooms and open breezeways. The large rooms, airy and quiet, are in need of fresh paint. The whole building has an atmosphere of faded elegance. There is no silver, no porcelain, no flowers. In the large dining room, in a niche on the side wall stands a huge painted drain tile filled with fluffy branches of field cotton.

Across the entry courtyard there is a small seventeenth century chapel. Inside in the gloom a massive dark hand-carved altar fills the whole end of the building. The chapel must have been here since the ranch was built by the first owners, the Jesuits. The cool darkness is almost mystical.

I am disappointed not to have seen the Nasca Lines today. It would be nice to be able to be in two places at once. But at the end of the day, there is an announcement that there will be one pictograph visible on shore as the ship leaves port. We are late in sailing. I am dancing around in frustration for fear the light will disappear before we get to the right location. Finally, in the dim twilight, a great candelabra appears on a hillside. It may be a candle holder or a giant stylized plant with opposing branches. No-one is quite sure of the significance or method of construction of these lines in the desert. They lead to speculation as we lean on the rail and watch intriguing Peru disappear in the gloom.

CHILE—ARICA

JANUARY 17TH The only outlet to the sea for the country of Bolivia is Arica, so this is a busy port. Fish meal is the chief export. It perfumes the air. We are told there are no sewers in this third world country. Huge drain tiles transport raw sewage out to sea. The Atacama desert surrounds the port. It never rains here, so houses are cheaply built, only giving privacy and shelter from the sun.

We visit a golf course, unlike any we have ever seen. Fairways and greens are laid out over rolling sand dunes. Golfers carry a pad with them so that they can have a firm area from which to hit the ball. Asphalt forms the surfaces of the greens, giving a smooth roll toward the cup. The golf course hands out cards with layouts of holes and distances just like any normal course would. Golfers are the same everywhere: they will find a way to play the game, no matter what the circumstances.

* * * * *

Marion Zimmerman has her attractive children, Gayle and Jerry and their friendly spouses, on board. She gives a cocktail party in the Crow's Nest to introduce them. Gayle is a younger version of her mother, with the same gentian blue eyes. She is a former District Governor of Rotary, so she and Pete find a lot to talk about. Jerry and Peggy run the family vineyard in Lodi, California. I am intrigued with the idea of trying to buy wine made from juice from their vineyard when we get back to Florida. If it is not readily available in the liquor store, we can get in touch with them at jerryfry@mohrfry.com. The younger generation leaves the ship in Buenos Aires, but Marion is on for the full cruise.

CHILE—COQUIMBO

JANUARY 19TH This is one of those unknown places: it sounds terrific in the brochure and turns out to be the shore trip from hell. There is too much walking, we are fed too many facts and there are several short stops with not much to see—a generally bad four hours. We visit a seedy museum with an original Easter Island Moai statue. Other exhibits are poorly lit. Old birds with decrepit feathers are stuffed together in small cases. The aisles are crowded; the museum is hot. We return to the entrance where we find hand-knit hats for sale and buy six of them to take to the grandchildren.

The last stop of the trip isn't any more successful. We visit a Pisco distillery where the process is shown in such a noisy environment we can scarcely hear the explanation. After traipsing through the halls, we are led to the tasting room where various flavors of Pisco are offered. Rather than a decent taste, the samples are offered in communion-size cups. We don't like the citrus and spice flavors anyway. The cups are being grabbed by so many hands, we give up and go outside to find the bus. Some trips just don't work out.

* * * * *

I have seen a ghost on the Rotterdam. She is a lean, tall, older woman with grey hair, who is always walking away from me down the long corridor of Verandah deck. Every time I see her, perhaps eight or ten sightings so far, she is dressed in the same rust-colored fitted long jacket and an ankle-length print orange and black skirt.

Her shoes are slippers. The key slot in her cabin door always has the Do Not Disturb card in place. Her excursions out into the world seem to focus on carrying trays of half-eaten food and dishes down the hall to the elevator landing area where she puts them on the floor. I don't believe she ever leaves her cabin for more than that, although once she did take a swing through the laundry. I was reading there in the cool environment, waiting for clothes to dry. I had a sense she was taking a constitutional loop around the halls before going back to her cabin.

There are other eccentric passengers on the ship, including the Mad Hatter. She is a skinny little slip of a grey-haired woman who brought twenty-eight hats on board. She wears a different homemade hat each day and evening. Sometimes bright green tendrils of seaweed straggle down from the top of her head, surrounding her face with a watery halo. Another time it may be a large red top-hat with three foot peacock feathers that annoy her neighbors. She has a cheese-head hat, like those Wisconsin football fans wear. Another hat displays a rabbit head and body, with floppy ears and pink eyes. One is twenty-four-inches in diameter and ten-inches thick—a cheeseburger. Rumor says she makes these wonders. They do help her stand out from the crowd.

Another character is Bobaloo. Think of the skinniest, wiriest little man you have ever seen, make him a 72-year-old Vietnamese and a janitor in a school in California, give him boundless energy, a love of dancing, and a genius for charming the crew into parting with items of their clothing, and you will be able to visualize the man. He saves every penny he can scrape up, stashes it with his travel agent and travels as soon as he has enough for a segment. He has apparently been on other portions of world cruises because he is familiar to lots of those who go every year.

Kissing Annie is a belt high bit of a woman who has different hair colors for day and evening. By daytime she is topped with iron grey curls covered by an embroidered and mirrored cap from India. By night she sports a perfectly styled blonde wig. Her upper surface is the first part most of us see, so her head coverings are important. Annie is a fixture on Holland America Line and everyone knows her, especially the entertainers. She makes a practice of inviting them to dinner at her table in the dining room. The Maitre de visits her table every single night to be sure all is well.

On every Cruise Specialists' clients' door there is a black and white paper penguin, about 18" tall. They are made of expandable tissue like wedding bells from a party store. My first thought was that they will be defaced or stolen, but neither happens. The penguins remain in place, white tummies protruding into the halls. They cause a little confusion when a steward carries a breakfast tray into the cabin, but it is fun to look through the halls and see how many there are. There are three escorts from the agency on board to help with our problems, Tom Mullen, Leslie Schoonderbeek and John Heimerdinger. They are available to answer questions every sea-day morning from nine to eleven.

CHILE—VALPARAISO

JANUARY 20TH We met John and Janet Herrigel in the first week we were here. They are friends of Lou and Jane Schaeffer who circled South America with us ten years ago. Janet is tall and elegant. John has a twinkle in his eyes and a good sense of humor. We share the day in Valparaiso by accident. We all arrive on the dock about the same time and agree to taxi together to Vina del Mar.

The resort town is shady and pleasant when the taxi drops us at the town square. We walk for a few minutes and decide the most attractive diversion is the long line of horse drawn buggies. An hour-long ride behind the slowly clopping horse shows us the resort city with its substantial stone buildings and leafy streets. We visit all the sights, get some sun and have a great time. At one point we climb a long hill in four lanes of traffic, causing consternation to other drivers. Pete rides high on the front seat next to the driver so he really gets the forward view. The three of us are in the back, in deep seats, more aware of what is going on behind us. We agree we found a great way to spend the sunny afternoon.

* * * * *

We run into Janet Reed during lunch one day in the Lido. One of the attractions of the less formal cafeteria on the Lido Deck is the famous Holland America Bread Pudding, served for dessert at lunch time We feel better if we forego that temptation. Janet arrives at our table carrying two desserts and is not the least uncomfortable about eating both. She and her husband, Porter, are friends from four years ago. We tell her she can expect a surprise from him, for we saw him buy an armload of bright red carnations in the market today. Her eyes dance as she tries to guess what's coming.

Caroline and Ron Evans from St. Louis have a charming cocktail party in the Crow's Nest at the top of the ship. About forty of us join in toasting our good sense in taking this exciting cruise. Conversations are eager for we are all glad to be here, with such a long leisurely expanse of time ahead of us. The Evanses are gracious hosts. Small parties are a special delight because there is time to really visit with each of the guests.

CHILE—PUERTO MONTT

JANUARY 22ND We remember this place from ten years ago, a prosperous area with a temperate climate. I am glad the Atacama Desert is behind us, for the air was so dry, it made us cough and sneeze. Here, where it does rain, trees and flowers make the landscape look more familiar. Out in the countryside, the fields resemble western New York. This area was settled in the mid-1800s by German immigrants who made systematic order out of unruly nature. Rectangular fields with placid cows and healthy crops are a nice change after days of desert.

After a 25-minute bus ride, we visit Frutillar on the shores of Lake Llanquihue (pronounced Yankeeway). I hop off the bus to explore brick cobbled sidewalks. A short walk down to the lake passes prolific gardens and well-kept yards. The little brick houses are immaculate—I can almost see cheery-faced housewives sweeping front walks each morning. Surrounding each house are little yards where flowers top fences and give just a glimpse of the interior. At the foot of the street on this grey morning, in the distance across the lake, I see the Osorno volcano, snow-topped, silent, ominous.

Some spirit calls me to turn left and after walking a couple of blocks on the narrow sidewalk, I have a serendipitous experience. On the lake side of the road stands a tall Christmas tree shape, made of iron, hung with symbols of local interests. I can't decipher what each one means, but I see a violin, a piano, a man catching a huge fish, a cow and a stag, a church and a sailboat. Little profiles of a couple with flat hats and a long skirt on the woman echo the town's German heritage. The sign is like some we saw hanging in Black Forest villages telling of the trades practiced in the town. A visit to a charming and unexpected place like this one makes all the shore trips that turn out to be zero worthwhile.

* * * * *

Never before have we been in a country that overthrew its elected government by such a close margin of days. Ten short days ago we were in Manta, Ecuador, where we learned about their economic crisis. Our guide told us that they had no welfare programs: if you want to eat, you have to work. She talked about an average monthly wage of $200 and how that amount didn't cover necessities. That was the same place where the thin little boy made a point of saying "Thank you" for my four-dollar purchase.

Today the paper says the Indians rioted in Quito and the military took charge, replacing the elected President with the Vice President. We, who are tourists, often do not understand the significance of what we hear and see.

CHILE—PUNTA ARENAS

JANUARY 25TH This is one of the magical places of the world. The tip of South America, described by Bruce Chatwin in *In Patagonia,* has lured me vicariously for years. He paints a word picture of sheep ranches in the area and the cool grey year-round climate, the towns and some of the people.

From here passengers can take a flight over Antarctica, as we did ten years ago, but now that we plan to visit the seventh continent by ship, I can't think why anyone would want to go by plane. We skip the trip to the penguin colony for the same reason. We expect to see plenty of them in a few days.

Jim Reid has talked in his enlightening lecture series about the history of Punta Arenas and in particular about a woman who was a local *grande dame* a hundred years ago. After her husband died, Sara Braun took over the family business. She made enough money in shipping and sheep to build the biggest house in town. I walk through the first floor, admiring high ceilings, Victorian furniture and florid wallpaper. On the street side, there is a greenhouse, now turned into an attractive dining room, with a live grape vine giving texture to the glass ceiling. Huge bunches of pale green iridescent grapes hang overhead. The house is a private club and a museum and it is well-maintained.

We visit the cemetery, an eerie place. The high pine hedges give me the feeling of being in a maze. All the mausoleums are built above ground, row after row of rococo stone grave chambers for the dead. The place is almost claustrophobic, so closely are the tombs lined up. Sara Braun donated a magnificent set of stained glass gates to the cemetery, on condition that they be used only once, when her corpse was carried through, and then they were to be locked for eternity. And so they were. Strange folks, these Punta Arenians.

* * * * *

During these days at sea, we are entertained and educated by a variety of performers. Col. James Reid is a friend from many cruises. His lectures are multi-media events, with slides, lecture and indigenous music. One of the favorite entertainers on HAL is back on board—Elliott Finkle. He plays the piano with the vigor that only a 6'7" giant can generate. We never miss one of his performances. Gail Sheehy is with us for a couple of weeks, a pretty woman who always wears turquoise to set off her reddish hair. She speaks about her new book, *Hillary's Choice*. She has lots to tell and a political evaluation of that woman who is running for the Senate in New York.

* * * * *

With the lift of surprise, like opening a Christmas gift, we fling open the drapes each morning. Charles Darwin sailed here: the Beagle Channel, south of the Straits of Magellan. It is more intimate than the wide vistas of Magellan, more single-directional. We sail east, having exited the Strait during the night. Our goal is Ushuaia, the southernmost city in the world.

"No birds, no bees, no leaves on the trees. No wonder, November": the old childhood poem captures the scene in the northern hemisphere. Here, in the Southern, it is summer, January, but the thought remains. Heavy grey clouds obliterate the mountain tops. Rock cliffs edge the shore. Stubby pines cover the steep surfaced mountain slopes. Frothing white surf edges the shoreline. Wisps of mist glide past. Loneliness is all around. Nature owns this world; it is not made for man. There are neither ships nor any sign of habitation. We are alone in the gloom. Captain Dijk said at a cocktail party last night that either he or First Officer Arjen van der Loo would be on the bridge all night in these narrow channels. Rotterdam is an enormous ship to sail through such closed spaces.

Suddenly rock-scoured peaks lined with gleaming snow glide from behind the enclosing banks. The ship sails with relentless grace. We move with ease due to the recent invention of global positioning instruments. Sonar and radar, wit and experience all add to the skills of the men on the bridge.

ARGENTINA—USHUAIA

JANUARY 26TH Mountains, mountains, mountains. Tierra del Fuego is as peaky as Switzerland. Pointed black mountains with hanging glaciers and snow-lined valleys surround the tiny city of Ushuaia. Flat shoreline turns into scrub-lined low hills; behind the town, part way up the hills, the tree line ends. Mountains rise like inverted ice cream cones in a row. It is mid-summer here, the temperature is 45° and gusty winds increase the chill. Ushuaia used to be a penal colony for Argentina. Do the people who live here now feel imprisoned in this isolated place at the bottom of the world?

We land at a bright pastel town, tiny against the mountain grandeur. Low buildings are painted vibrant shades: chrome yellow, forest green, bright blue, dark rose. It's as if the residents want to make a cheery atmosphere with color.

Rarely do we dock right in the middle of town, where we can walk to the shops, but here the town is small and there is only one dock. Tied up near us are the Bremen, an adventure explorer ship that sails to Antarctica, a cargo ship from Panama and three or four other vessels. A dozen oil storage tanks line the hills. Ushuaia claims to be the southernmost city in the world.

Our goal today is exploring the recently finished last segment of the Pan American Highway that runs down through the Andes to this town on Tierra del Fuego. We board a bus for a scenic alpine drive. The buses roll out of town on the three-mile-long paved highway and then for two more hours we travel a brand new dirt road. Sunshine lights the peaks as we climb higher into the

Andes. Mountains and glaciers envelop us. The air is fresh and crisp. A stop at an overlook gives us a sense of our small size compared to the gigantic peaks of this mighty mountain chain. We head on to Lake Escondido, two hours away, a so-called lost lake.

When we arrive at the lake on the high plateau, there is a feeling of relief at being able to get out of the bus. A new rustic building faces the lake shore where pedal powered boats are for rent. There is a rusting dock and a shelter with benches and picnic tables. We choose a seat in the sun, open our tote bag and spread napkins over the bench. Sandwiches, fruit and cheese from room service are unpacked. We share with everyone who comes along. Jim Reid, the lecturer, who is trying to maintain his slim shape so all his double breasted suits still fit, selects one almond for his lunch. Others with more normal appetites join us and the picnic feeds Craddocks, McNeeses and us. Other passengers eat from the Argentine buffet at the highway restaurant.

After a brief pause, we climb back in the buses and return the way we came. The magnificent Andes mountains surround us for the whole day. As we retrace our way to Ushuaia, knowing this is the last shore trip for a week, our thoughts turn away from this continent and to the most spectacular and anticipated adventure of the trip—Antarctica.

ARGENTINA—CAPE HORN

But first comes Cape Horn. We were in this area ten years ago, but then we sailed west to east through the Straits of Magellan and never saw the fabled Cabos Hornos. The tip of South America is said to have the roughest water in the world. Sailing books tell wild tales of ships spending months rounding the Horn. We look forward to seeing the famous rocks but at the same time expect to find rough weather.

Cape Horn is off our starboard side at seven AM on Thursday, January 27th. We have a grey, rainy but reasonably calm day to meet this infamous place. Here three oceans converge, the Southern, the Atlantic and the Pacific.

The Cape was first rounded by Isaac Le Maire and the Dutch Schouten brothers on January 29, 1615, 385 years and three days ago. Sailors of that day were searching for a passage to the spice islands because the route around the Cape of Good Hope in Africa was dangerous due to pirates and Arab raiders. When they passed the southernmost cluster of rocks, land fell away to the north and they knew they had done it.

As often happens, my concern is unnecessary. The ship is able to linger, almost lovingly, with smooth seas. When we sail away it is with a sense of omission, as if something were left out, as if the fabled reputation eluded us. Now the rain descends and the skies close in. We pound our way south through increasingly rough seas.

ANTARCTICA

One of the things Holland America does best is present us with a variety of information and intellectual challenges. An Antarctic Experience, as the ship calls it, our lecture series for this highlight of the cruise, is graced by four men who are specialists in their fields. Dr. Bernard Stonehouse is the premier authority in the world on penguins. Dr. Don Walsh, former submarine commander and oceanographer, has been down deeper in the sea than any other living person. Captain Lawson Brigham, from the Coast Guard Academy, is an expert on Antarctic exploration. The fourth member of the team is Captain Pat Toomey, the finest ice pilot in the world, a Canadian who leads convoys through the ice in the Arctic and on the Great Lakes. He is a spare angular fellow, with steely eyes, accustomed to command. He tells us the tale of a novice captain who kept jumping out of line in a convoy he was guiding through the ice. The other ship needed to be rescued several times as a result. Captain Toomey told the novice that if he got crosswise to the line again, he would drive his icebreaker right through his ship, somewhere between the stacks and the bow. A voice from way back in the convoy came on the radio and drawled, "You can believe him. He'd do it!" The troublemaker heeded the warning and stayed in line.

* * * * *

January 28th We wake to see white cliffs moving by our verandah, endless convoluted whiteness, stretching to the horizon in both directions. The passengers tumble out of the warmth to stand in awe at the ice and the black rocks sliding past, with cliffs towering up to a thousand feet above our heads on both sides of a narrow channel. Where the shoreline stretches away to the distance, long folds of white slopes recede in layers to infinity. Sharp peaks of black rock make up the continent. A mere eight percent of the rock isn't covered with snow and ice. Huge white shelves meet the sea where rivers of ice break off. Small icebergs dot the surface of the sea.

On an iceberg a dozen yards long, little soldiers stand erect on guard: penguins—perhaps Adelie or Chinstrap—and here and there in the water a hunting leopard seal. The seals eat penguins, and they keep a constant watch out for their next catch.

It is an austere, cold environment. Man is the only mammal that can survive in Antarctica. There are mosses, and lichens and four species of spiders. How do they exist? This is midsummer. Pete compares the temperature to a trip to the seawall at Lake Erie in mid-winter. Lecturers point out special sights and relay information as we slide through the silent waterways.

Two thirds of the earth's land is in the Northern Hemisphere. Eighty percent of this Southern Hemisphere is covered by water. Antarctica, the seventh continent, is larger than the United States. We hear that the ozone hole above the continent is the same size as the United States. We are cautioned about sunscreen and wearing hats.

Parkas and windbreakers, gloves, scarves, knitted hats from Chile, pashmina shawls, and cargo pants are the uniform of the day but, most surprising, we see shorts and bare legs on Ed Glasman. He's the guy who daily occupies "teak beach" at the back end of the suite deck. Now that we have been at sea for a few weeks, his skin is a nice homey shade of molasses.

Moe Craddock has a wonderful toy—an Iridium phone. It has the capacity to make connections to satellites from anywhere in the world. Pete stands on the back outside deck and calls Dan at the office from Antarctica. Both of them are delighted with the unique phone call. Dan is astonished to hear from us when we are in such a remote place.

Before noon Lynn and Chuck Anderson entertain Table M with Bloody Marys at the Lido pool bar. A movable roof, made of clear panels, slides over the pool, making this a perfect place to watch the scenery. When the naturalist, Dr. Stonehouse, calls out a sight, we can rush to either side for a glimpse. Feeding humpback whales, leopard seals and penguins all cause a race for the windows. As we sail along in calm sunny seas, the warm atmosphere of the Lido pool is in sharp contrast to the snow and cold outside. One man is swimming. Several others are napping (they will nap through anything!) as we sail through the amazing scenery.

We cruise past Anvers Island, through the Gerlach Strait, down the Lemaire Channel, into Paradise Harbor (where our enormous ship must turn around and go out the narrow channel we came in). Mountains covered with snow pass so close on both sides we feel as if we could reach out and touch them. Here and there, God, with a paint brush of deep turquoise blue, has frosted fissures and cracks and shoreline cliffs of ice with bright color.

We are not the first ship-load of tourists to come here, but we are the first full-size cruise ship, with more than fifteen hundred passengers and crew to visit. It is not long since the film, *Titanic*, and many of us consider the fact that the Rotterdam hull is not ice-strengthened. But we have a perfect day: calm wind, calm water, blue sky, blinding sunshine. One of the experts tells us this weather occurs just five percent of the time. Rotterdam luck holds again. Our ship glides past a changing landscape of ice all day long, as her passengers take deep breaths of cold fresh air and revel in the vast frozen landscape.

About four PM the atmosphere changes. A fresh breeze begins to buffet the ship. The sky develops that luminous gray glow that precedes snow in western New York. Increasing wind means we pop in and out of our verandah door, looking or photographing in brief spurts, then quickly return to the warmth and shelter of the cabin. The ship begins to tremble with the strong wind.

Ruth Diamond, Pete and I sit in the empty Lido as the sky slowly darkens. As this magical day changes to twilight, we sail past Elephant Island where Shackleton and his men found refuge. The forbidding look of the island makes us wonder how those twenty-three men managed to stay alive for three and a half months until they were rescued. The film, *South,* is shown on board. The original movie film from 1914-1916, taken by the expedition's photographer, makes the story come alive. Dr. Brigham says we can buy it from Milestone Films at 1-800-603-1104.

We sail past Deception Island, a caldera where the water is warm enough for swimming and the sands are too hot for walking with bare feet. We have had such a perfect day that if tomorrow is less beautiful, we will have no complaint. A sudden storm frosts the windows as light disappears. Sleet flies horizontally, just as it does in western New York. You have to experience Antarctica to feel the immensity of it. We are thrilled to have spent a dozen hours navigating these pristine channels.

* * * * *

This is our second day in Antarctica. I am up at 4 AM when daylight arrives, but I go back to bed to sleep until seven. At that hour the ship's naturalist wakes us with promises of icebergs and more penguins. We open the curtains to see immense flat glacial chunks, tilting at assorted angles, sailing on a grey sea beneath a blue sky, filling the horizon. The bergs tower a hundred feet above the waterline, which means another seven hundred feet below, invisible, an ominous danger below the surface of the sea. The great size of the icebergs makes me think of office buildings and football fields for comparison. We must be seeing a hundred icebergs at a time, like independent ladies, all present in a dignified way. There is a certain resemblance in demeanor between these icebergs and the ladies of the Shakespeare Club back home. The sun is shining brightly, the sea is calm, as we sail among these magnificent beauties.

Surrounding us are chunks of the whitest white I have ever seen, set against the grey of the sea, the black of the shore and pale blue sky. Great geometric shapes float nearby. As the ship glides past, the tops of the giant blocks of ice are at eye level with us, ten stories above sea level. It is as if some Godly Monopoly player has set giant house-size slabs on a calm sea to watch the slowly changing relationships. The only relief from the penetrating whiteness is a cast of color from the algae inside the ice—here red—there blue, against acres and miles of blinding white. This is the whitest landscape on the earth, blinding, pervading, everywhere white, austere, endless. All possible variations on trapezoid shapes are here. There is an iceberg for each of the fifteen hundred persons on this ship, right here in Hope Bay of the Weddell Sea.

The only relief to the blinded eye is the small cluster of red buildings that make up Esperanza Station—the Argentine research station. I searched the Internet for information about this site and had been sent some charts by the U.S. Coastal Service. We sail past the actual installation. Photos from space cannot do it justice. Flat red buildings are scattered along a low shoreline under towering mountains in a quiet bay.

There is a small black inflatable boat on the bay, the only other manmade thing besides the station and us, as far as the eye can see. Researchers watch our intrusion into their quiet world for a few minutes, and then, as if inspired by a sudden idea, they show us they are glad to see us by tearing forward at full speed, circling the gigantic invader from another world. By the time they finish their complete loop around the sedate Rotterdam, the rails are lined with cheering and waving passengers.

Ranging up the hill behind the small research station are thousands of penguins. When man invades, nature persists and usually wins. This slope was the birds' historic breeding ground before scientists arrived. It will be again when the intruders have been satisfied and are gone.

Penguins come in all sizes. They are unable to fly, but they swim with speed—rushing through the water in sleek arcs. Some of the tiniest ones are the size of flying fish. We didn't see the Emperors, the largest at almost four feet tall. They live in another part of Antarctica. But since we have Dr. Stonehouse on board, we see lots of slides and learn about their intriguing habits. Females lay eggs and immediately pass them to the males and then they depart, walking or land surfing, across the ice to the nearest water to feed. That trip may cover as much as a hundred miles. The males incubate the eggs for six weeks in their pouches and on their feet. They don't eat at all during this period. The females return within a day or so of the chick's hatching, with a cropful of food for the baby. If they don't time their return just right, the chicks will starve. The males depart for their feeding cycle and by the time chicks are big enough to require both parents to feed them constantly, the ice has melted so that the food supply is close by. Among all the thousands of pairs of dads and chicks, the mothers can always find the right chick.

The greatest threat to a penguin's existence is the leopard seal. Each seal eats ten to twelve adult penguins a day and then loiters at the foot of an icy slope, catching penguins for sport. The seals are hunted in turn by orcas or killer whales, who cruise in packs nearby. A suitable payoff, I think, for hunting these appealing little birds.

Besides the birds and the seals, we see humpback whales, sixty to eighty feet long, black and sleek, flipping their tail flukes at us as they head for the depths. What a magical day!

The brightness of the sun, the whiteness of the ice, the eye-blinding quality of the light all stuns us. The atmosphere is so dry that our hands turn to sandpaper; noses are as dry as soda crackers. Cold and wind cut through every layer of clothing. We marvel at our good luck in such perfect weather for these two exhilarating days.

After leaving Antarctica I learn that we got within sixty miles of the Antarctic Circle. Our latitude reading was 65°08' south. The source of that information was Captain Toomey. He describes three ways to define Antarctica. The Antarctic Circle is where there is a day each year with no daylight and a day with no darkening.

The Antarctic Convergence is where warm subtropical water and cold subantarctic water collide. It is drawn as a circle around the continent. The third definition of Antarctica is political: the area to which the Antarctic treaty applies based on geographic definition. We crossed two of the defined boundaries. We have not touched foot on the seventh continent, but we feel we have been there and seen it.

* * * * *

During this voyage, we eat too much, we drink too much and we enjoy every minute of it. The wonderful menus that are offered for dinner have us salivating by lunch time. We can study a menu near the dining room each day so that we know our choices for appetizer, soup, salad, entree and dessert in advance. One night a former ship's doctor comments, as we both take a chocolate from the tray in the Explorer's Lounge, "There are four basic food groups on this ship—fat, sugar, salt and alcohol." She is lean as a rail and clearly manages her intake well. We are beginning to show the effects of the wonderful food in our waistlines.

* * * * *

On Super Bowl Sunday, the 30th of January, a long arm of the United States reaches out toward us. The movie theater is set up with big screen TV. Outside in the entry, there are hamburgers and beer. The men delight in being able to see the game as it happens. This is the first time Rotterdam has been able to offer this attraction to its passengers.

For nearly a month the ship has been dawdling around in a couple of time zones, but now we really begin our voyage east. In 1996, before our first World Cruise, we had to look at the map to discover that the world is divided into 24 time zones. Now, traveling east means a lost hour of sleep every third night or so for the rest of the trip. Stewards who work until midnight in the Lido and have to tend breakfast by eight in the dining room will have trouble adjusting.

Most nights we don't leave the dinner table until ten o'clock. The entertainment after dinner lasts until eleven. If we have to get up by 6:30 to make an early shore excursion, the end result is a pretty short night. Some of us have tried suggesting that having the time change occur in the daytime would be a better idea but the Captain is not convinced.

ARGENTINA—BUENOS AIRES

FEBRUARY 2ND In all we have spent a week at sea with our great Antarctic adventure, so Buenos Aires is a welcome sight. Pete and I sign up for three shore excursions. When we were here ten years ago, we spent all our time visiting our former Argentine exchange student, staying at his house, meeting his lawyer wife and two-year-old son and visiting his family. This time we have written Miguel and not heard a word in reply. We go ahead and arrange our plans, wondering if we will see him at all.

The highlights of the city tour in the morning show us elegant subdivisions with gorgeous landscaping, and the less luxurious older part of town called La Boca. Here buildings are flamboyant with bright paint. We don't get back to the ship until one o'clock and there, waiting for us near the gangplank, are Miguel and Patricio. It is fun showing them the ship, the Lido for lunch, the pool, our cabin and some of the more dramatic public spaces. Miguel videotapes everything he sees so he can take it home and show his family. In the intervening years, he and his wife have been divorced and she is remarried. They share Patricio, two weeks at a time. The boy seems well adjusted and bright. His English is quite good although he is shy for a few moments about using it. We spend the afternoon together, a satisfying visit.

After dinner there is a Shore Excursion to a Tango show. Passengers file into long rows of chairs ranging along a narrow stage. Pete and I sit next to the stage at a plank table that runs its length. The excitement builds as the lights dim and dancers appear. The women wear sleek dresses of clinging cloth and have pasted-down shiny hair. The men are lithe like cats, dressed in tight pants, with black hats tipped at jaunty angles. Their high heeled boots move two feet from our faces. I pull my drink back for fear someone will kick it. The dancers whirl and insinuate themselves into each other's space, clinging, then parting. Sensuous music sets the pace of the dance. We, who know nothing about tango, are cheering and clapping as the performance progresses. By the end of the evening, we see the tango as the symbol of culture in Argentina that it is.

* * * * *

The next day we drive to Fiesta Gaucha at a historic horse ranch in the countryside. Six swarthy, stocky men in white shirts, and tan baggy pants with black boots and hats entertain us with an hour of horse wrangling tricks. They gather and gallop and wheel their herds of a dozen horses with grace and precision. They show their skill at "hands off" control of their horses by riding full speed toward a tiny ring suspended from overhead frames. A small twig held steady at eye level as they stand up in their stirrups is hooked into the ring when they pass below. The competition among the men grows urgent. We film and cheer their steadiness and control.

A barbecue lunch with free flowing wine and a musical performance complete the day. The food is smoky from the barbecue pit, and we are hungry after all the fresh air. There are generous amounts of sausage, chicken and tough beef. The sausage is a blood sausage. I try it and find it mushy and black tasting. Not a favorite. After lunch there is a performance of Argentine singing and more tango. This show makes us appreciate even more the style and grace of last night.

Jackie and Beth leave the ship today, on their way home after a month with us. Charlotte and Tim Nault get on board. She is a former nurse, mother of nine. Tim is an architect who has quarter-size blue eyes which he uses expressively. We met them three years ago on the maiden voyage of Rotterdam from Barcelona, Spain, to Florida. They have traveled frequently in the interval and are old hands at shipboard sports and navy talk. They join the eight of us at dinner.

TRISTAN DA CUNHA

We are racing east through a dark grey sea, under low-hanging clouds toward an improbable place: the island of Tristan da Cunha. The Atlantic has been calm for the last four days, since we left Buenos Aires. The current is with us. We clip along at a nice twenty-two knot pace. These long sea days give World Cruisers a chance to rest, to get deep into whatever book we are reading or to spend lots of time at exercise classes or doing laundry. We have had so many days at sea in a row—six of them in Antarctica, and now six more to Capetown. But we all know what is coming: Africa, with its assault on all our senses. This period of hibernation readies us for the ten exciting days to follow.

Tristan da Cunha is the top of a 10,000 foot ocean floor volcano that has collapsed in on itself and is usually dormant. It sits in the south Atlantic, a thousand miles from everything. High cliffs surround the island and the isolation makes it a forbidding place and yet three hundred people live here. No plane can land, no help or supplies can come except by sea, and the sea in this region often is too rough for anyone to get ashore. One day in three may be calm enough for boats.

We sit in the land of kippered herrings and eggs Benedict, of filet mignon and hot hors d'oeuvres, of Belgian chocolates and fresh flowers, and watch quietly as this austere piece of earth slides by our balcony. We are grateful to be here on this ship and not there. What is it like to be a child in such a place, to have books be the only escape? I wonder if there are creeks and hills and valleys? Where does fresh water come from? Are there bugs and salamanders? What about flowers? If some of us have trouble eating with the same six or eight people every night for dinner, how must it be to live with the same three hundred people all your life?

I take a quick swing through the cafeteria to see if the promised ship-wide commentary can be heard there. In the midst of the aromas of breakfast bacon and coffee, half the people are sitting on the wrong side of the ship and won't even see the island. How can they be so disinterested?

The first time we were here four years ago we paused on the south side of Tristan da Cunha to deliver some parts for a transoceanic sailboat that had broken down. We saw only high cliffs and the small boat that came out to meet us. The little boat and its four men dressed in orange wet suits looked forlorn as they headed back to the dreary shore.

This visit we pass near the north shore. The cliffs do not drop straight to the sea. They are inland a little, just enough to allow a small strip of level green land next to the sea, a half mile deep and four miles long. The clouds clear for a moment and the whole little village is warmed by a flat bright rainbow that seems as wide as it is high. The settlement has a few dozen houses, a warehouse or two, a hospital and a school. It would be wonderful to understand how such isolation can be an attraction. They must have a splendid library. I wonder if they are available on the Internet. The sense of isolation is enhanced because we know first hand how far away land is from this place.

I wonder what sort of people live here, what their priorities are. What an incomprehensible place.

SOUTH AFRICA—CAPETOWN

FEBRUARY 11TH A sharp smell of fish, banks of low-lying dark clouds, a rosy glow in the sky with one shining morning cloud hanging over the tall flat topped mountains greet us in Capetown, South Africa. In spite of four time changes in one week at sea, I pop out from a sound sleep at 5:30 to see land. When you have been at sea as long as we have, with only an albatross to accompany us, a new continent is a welcome sight.

We stay a day and a half in this city that once was called the "tavern of the seas." The Cape of Good Hope was discovered by Vasco da Gama for Portugal in the early 1600s; it became a reprovisioning stop for sailors on their way to India and the spice islands. The Dutch established what they called a "factory" here to grow fresh fruits and vegetables to feed the sailors who had been at sea for months. It was known that fresh food and lemons would prevent the scurvy that caused teeth to fall out, joints to swell and men to die.

Gene Masica says that the British discovered that rum would prevent scurvy and that is why British sailors have been drinking rum ever since. I thought they were called "limeys" for the limes they sucked for the same purpose. He likes to tease at the dinner table.

On a clear day the flat shape of Table Mountain can be seen a hundred miles out to sea, welcoming every ship that sails around the Cape and Point Agulhas, the actual southernmost land in Africa. Rafts of white-striped black ducks greet us as we sail into the harbor. Pancake-shaped Robben Island, where Nelson Mandela was imprisoned, stands at the entrance. He spent twenty years in prison during the apartheid period of the seventies and eighties. A less exclusionary government now is holding "forgiveness courts" where former guards can admit their crimes of those earlier days and be absolved. Some old hates have been aired. South Africa is a country with huge reserves of gold and diamonds and thirty-five million blacks who have less than a third grade education. The literacy rate is low and the unemployment rate is fifty percent, with another ten percent being employed part-time. Five million whites control the economy. Three million "coloreds" are the result of the blending of the cultures. One million Indians keep to themselves, maintain their own culture and run the small trade shops. The days of Afrikaner supremacy have been gone for half a dozen years.

Cape of Good Hope Nature Reserve is our goal today, the first of several game runs. Africa holds such a variety of animals that we are going to try a game drive at each port and hope to see different species each time. Driving through Clifton and on to Seaforth gives an idea of the countryside. Most amazing to us are the fortified homes we pass. There are tall fences and heavy steel gates around moderate size houses. Each gatepost bears a large sign that warns of vicious dogs and states that in case of emergency, an armed response will occur. As the guide drones on, we try to sense what is beneath the surface facts. One statistic stands out—last year South Africa recorded more than a million rapes. Residents can buy rape insurance. Combine this with the fact that more than a third of the population has either HIV or AIDS. Statistics predict that in the next decade there will be millions of children orphaned by AIDS in the area.

Lunch is at a restaurant high above the sea. We meet Charlie and Marie Steinke and enjoy their company at the breezy open air tables. After lunch I find raku' African animals in charming patchwork designs for the grandkids. There are an ostrich, a baboon, a lion, an elephant, a giraffe, and a rhino in yellow, green, blue and pink. They are heavy to carry but will be no trouble when we get back to the ship. A ship's passenger can carry and store anything for the trip home. Julia, from the Internet Café, is even buying furniture as we go. She has several carved chairs delivered to the ship today.

On our drive through the game preserve we see baboons in families and troops and singles, cavorting alongside the road. We are warned to keep our windows closed for the baboons can be trouble if they get inside the bus. There are huge wild ostriches in the distance, down by the seashore. We see a grysbok and a rhebok, both rare and nearly extinct these days.

After the animal run, we visit Groat Constantia, one of the most famous South African winery estates. The neat fields lead to substantial Dutch colonial buildings, manicured gardens and vineyards. Pete sits on a stone bench while I walk through the old manor house and admire the rooms. A fine life style must have been enjoyed in these halls. This South Africa is far removed from the slums and filth of the native settlements. With such extreme contrasts, it is no wonder they still have serious problems.

SOUTH AFRICA—DURBAN

FEBRUARY 14TH Valentine's Day The low plain where Durban lies is frosted with grey clouds. We rise at six to go on tour by seven-fifteen. A modest number of skyscrapers cluster on the flats. Anchored container ships wait for their turn to offload at the pier. The sandy brown water is calm. Everything hangs under a heavy load of humidity and the smell of cooking oil. Do ports have different smells that depend on the ethnic background of the residents? Do I smell the ghee that the million Indian residents use to cook their food? No fish odors predominate here, just oil and spices.

Our bus ride to Pietermaritzburg from Durban takes about two hours. We see and hear about the Voortrekkers, the Dutch who were driven out of Capetown by the British nearly three hundred years ago. In Pietermaritzburg we drive by a sturdy brown stone Voortrekker house from the 1700's.

Soon we are driving down a dirt road to Game Valley Nature Reserve. Lunch includes delicious homemade rolls, pate´, salads, beef, chicken in gravy with bones and skin, rice, vegetable lasagna and apple or chocolate pudding with ice cream. The main attraction at lunch is the family of warthogs who populate the lawn, right outside the open windows where we are served. They are semi-tame, which means we cannot approach them very closely before they raise their tails straight into the air, snort and turn and run. The old boar hog is huge and lazy, snuggling down for an afternoon nap in the shade of a tree, confident of his superiority. His six inch tusks are white curved weapons.

After lunch twenty of us clutch the rails in the back of an open Land Rover truck, and drive through herds of impala, blesbok, and gnu or wildebeest. We catch sight of a white rhino family, who occasionally take a dip in the swimming pool at the restaurant. There are seven giraffes in a small wood, stretching their slender necks to nibble leaves from the tops of the trees. What a satisfying afternoon.

Our guide today has been a tall man who wears shorts, boots, a bush jacket and bush hat. He is about fifty, with a handlebar mustache. As he describes the political scene, we learn he is a national guide, credentialled to work in other African countries, including Kenya, Zimbabwe and Tanzania. When we ask pointed questions, he talks about tolerance and the desire for inclusion of all segments of the population. In the last six years the African National Congress has been the ruling party. The homelands policy which threatened every black with deportation to an unfamiliar place has ended as has daily curfew for blacks. Blacks are now encouraged to vote; their voice in the democratic process is South Africa's hope for the future.

Calling places by British or Afrikaans names has ended. For example, the province of Natal has been renamed KwaZulu Natal—a more respectful name reflecting the history of the area. I ask the guide if his apparently balanced assessment of South Africa's future is his own opinion or if it is "government-speak." He admits he is a government spokesperson, but adds that he feels genuine hope for the future of South Africa. The people in the bordering countries evidently feel the same way for they are flooding into South Africa, looking for work and a better future than they can find in their own countries.

There is a lot of talk about the disappearance of wild animals from game preserves and national parks. Our guide explains that when hunger rules the land, the animals disappear. It is impossible for a native to believe that his one act of poaching can affect the gene pool in all of Africa. If it becomes a choice between man and beast, man is going to win. Man is the greater predator.

Emerging Africa is complex and contradictory. When white supremacists were overthrown in South Africa, six years ago, some whites fled. Investment declined. Now food production is half what it was during the colonial period. The management structure has collapsed. Blacks do not have enough education to run the farms. Middle management, those hired to supervise the labor force, has moved on to other work. There is no-one to take their place. While food self sufficiency has declined, the birth rate remains at an annual increase of three percent. Starvation will be the result. One of our speakers predicts that as long as upheaval and strife are common, animals will be in jeopardy. Hungry people do not count species extinction as important.

Across the valley, it begins to rain. Silver streaks pour down in a wide band from silver clouds into a broad silver lake, nestled between long low green hills. In some places the sun streaks through a space in the clouds to light the valley in squares of green and yellow. I see Hemingway's green hills stretching limitless to the distance. The soft hills and broad valleys described by Isak Dinesen lie in long rows. A bright orange and black Bishop's bird flashes in the brush and the whole universe vibrates with that one bright streak of color. The sweeping view across the valley as the silver rain moves through is the final blessing to a wonderful, though sobering day.

* * * * *

There is a big Valentine's Day party tonight. As a rule after a day ashore, we can wear casual clothes to dinner but not when a formal party is in the plans. We complain to each other as we dress in our best clothes. We are tired from the long day ashore. This party is an annual event. The Crow's Nest is reduced in size by so many ceiling decorations that tall men have to duck and dodge to move through the room. Elaborate displays of food decorate the back of the room. It is the largest party anyone will hold during the entire trip. More than two hundred guests are entertained generously by the hostesses—two sisters who take the World Cruise every year.

Later tonight the same decorations will provide atmosphere for the Officer's Ball. Single women can ask ship's officers to dance—an attraction for the late night party crowd. What a contrast there is between life on this ship and the problems of the countries we visit.

MADAGASCAR—NOSY BÉ

FEBRUARY 17TH This is an improbable place, one of those stops that make us speculate on why we even come here. Sweaty skinny black bodies press close to ours the minute we get off the tenders. Fingers touch and reach. Eyes plead. Mouths say "Dollar?" Little kids whine and wheedle with expert eyes that calculate our every response. Clots of older children exhibit ugly green lizards with pop eyes and ridges of scales down their backs, clinging tightly to the stick which displays them. A round-eyed black lemur has its long thin arms and legs wrapped tightly around its owner's neck.

It is hot, so hot that your clothes stick to your body. The uneven road is full of holes. It is lined with stalls displaying wood carvings, cutwork and embroidered lace tablecloths and beautiful seashells. We buy six shells as big as oranges for our grandchildren. There is a satiny pearl glow to the shells. Turquoise lines the spirals and there is a turquoise lip on the bottom. I get a table runner embroidered with black field workers for seven dollars, all handwork. We beat a hasty retreat to the ship from the heat, humidity, smells and mud. Perhaps the reason we come here is that the people are so poor and every dollar is appreciated so much.

When we return we discover the ship is being attacked by wooden outrigger canoes. Black kids jockey for position, paddling, two or three to a canoe, clustering around the stern of the ship like a swarm of dragonflies. The fragile boats are disreputable, many of them barely float. In some, the second person bails constantly. The ship's staff is clustered at the back rail of Main Deck, buying or swapping goods with the kids. Agreements are reached, money is lowered down in a Holland America bag on a rope, and bananas or carvings are raised up.

When we have our sail-away party this afternoon, the dozen people we invite for drinks have lots of fun throwing shampoo, lotion, soap with dollars in the box and candy to the eager hands below. Pete likes the looks of one young man. When he motions across his bare chest, Pete throws him his swim suit T shirt. I sail a purple sparkle-covered top hat at him, left over from the New Year's Eve celebration. Next he motions that he wants shoes. We shake our heads at that idea. Our guests have a good time as the bathroom is stripped bare of supplies.

As we sail away from Nosy Be´, I am satisfied with the thoughts of that young man in his new shirt and purple top hat, with some dollars in his pocket. We need to stop here, for the locals' benefit if not our own. We are reminded about how poor life can be.

* * * * *

After Madagascar, we meet a tropical cyclone off the coast, in the Mozambique channel. The rains that it produces cause great floods to the west of us. Water inundates towns and villages all over the flood plain of Mozambique. Our television is full of pictures of people being rescued from trees and rooftops by helicopter. The government sends out pleas for international help and money. Floods mean more refugees for South Africa and more threat to the wild life of the continent.

* * * * *

Among the passengers are a number of men who enjoy each other's company and are not interested in women and never will be. One fellow wears a dark helmet hairdo and appears to use mascara around his expressive eyes or maybe he has been tattooed with permanent eye makeup. Heavy gold chains decorate his chest under his open necked shirt. His aggressive insistent behavior dismays lots of passengers. Every evening during second seating cocktail hour, he and his principal friend are on the dance floor, asking women to dance. Their favorite venue is a small lounge that is interior to the ship, so it seems like a small island in the midst of pre-dinner activity. Guests on their way to dinner have to walk down the corridor past the open curtains where the dancers are on view. The men are attracted to women who flaunt their bodies as much as they do.

Unfortunately we must accept their rude behavior. One night two of them, for just the briefest instant, dance with each other in the Piano Bar. Pete is offended. He starts out of his chair, saying, "We'll have none of that around here." Luckily the guys didn't hear him and we move our drinks and ourselves to a lounge near the window. The Dutch have long been famous for their tolerance of alternative life styles. That can be understood if the behavior is unobtrusive, but when they kiss each other good night as they part, and are so assertive, they become annoying.

A few weeks ago Janet and John Herrigel proposed a Bloody Mary before lunch in their cabin. Arrayed on the counter were tomato juice, Worcestershire and hot pepper sauce and lemons. They supply the vodka or gin and pretzels. They assembled a nice number of plastic glasses with good capacity, borrowed from the Lido. The first Bloody Mary party is such a success that we have one every week, first in their cabin, then in ours. We have lunch in the Dining Room afterward. One day we see them walk by as we are eating with Tommie and Frank Matthews from Brantford, Ontario. We had met the Matthews by coincidence the previous day. Frank is an expert at "on line trading." Pete wants to find an Internet broker to do some of his trades for him. As Herrigels pass by, we invite them to join us for lunch and the six of us have a great time. Matthews will be included in future Bloody Mary parties.

TANZANIA—ZANZIBAR

FEBRUARY 19TH Fabled Zanzibar is sunny, hot and humid. For centuries this island dominated trade up and down the Swahili coast of Africa. When the island and the mainland joined together politically, Zanzibar became the "zan" in Tanzania. The island is flat and small, a relic split from the African continent millions of years ago. Creamy beaches are washed by milky blue water. The low roofs of Stonetown cluster at the right of the harbor. We visit on a blinding bright Saturday. Light is different here, more penetrating, more invasive.

The day doesn't start right. Passengers are ready to go ashore early, when a problem develops. As we sit in the theater, waiting for tender tickets, the loudspeaker tells us that the tenders cannot land. The tidal pull of the full moon, a beautiful sight at night from the ship's rails, is also a strong influence on the depth of the water. It's too shallow for tenders to go ashore. The few extra moments give me time to visit the Port Lecturer's Desk and ask some questions about where to find a bookstore in town. Frank Buckingham is a great source of all kinds of information on ports and shopping.

As a whole shipload of impatience sits idly by for four hours, the tide turns and begins to come in again. By the time we finally reach shore, all is well. We time our jump as the tender rises and falls, to be confronted with steps but no rails. Strong Indonesian arms lift us up. The cement block landing with eight or ten steps doesn't deserve to be called a dock. It is worn, uneven, crumbling and has no rails or bumpers to cushion the tender. We are suddenly in Zanzibar, plunged into a sea of clamoring black men.

Pete and I look for Juma Rashid, the driver we had when we were here four years ago. We had written him to expect us. But when we ask, the men on the dock all say he has gone off with other passengers. We waited on shipboard while I suppose he waited ashore. We run into Janet and John as they look for a taxi and they decide to join us. I want to find a bookstore to get some books on the history of this island.

A persistent fellow comes along, promising us the best taxi in all Zanzibar. We shrug our shoulders, pray, and go with him. He speaks good English, wears a white fez, has no upper front teeth and smiles at me all the time. Little pearls of saliva dance in the corners of his mouth. Sahel guarantees us he can interpret and deliver us in a cab to bookstores. He speaks with animation about other possibilities, the museums, spice farm, hotels, but we are fixed on our one goal.

The first bookstore we visit is in the Arab quarter of Stonetown, the oldest part of the city. It is an unassuming shop on a narrow street in a crowded part of the quarter. I am reluctant to get out of the taxi. Men are clustered around the doorway, reading the news of the day, taped to the doors of the shop. But in I go, to a shop that is like a closet off the street. The dark cave of the interior is crowded with men and display cases. Everything is locked up. An Arab shopkeeper blows an inch of dust off the yellowed books he tries to sell me—not what I had in mind. I beat a retreat as fast as I can and return to the taxi, asking to be taken to the shop on Gizenga Street that Frank Buckingham suggested.

After a short ride, we walk up a street and turn into a narrow shadowy alley lined with shops. A passageway zigzags between three story buildings that have mildewed walls and haphazard wooden shutters. The alley is quiet, for it is midday when all shops are closed and everyone has gone home to rest. Undaunted, Sahel marches up to a shuttered building and calls to an upper story window where a woman's head pops out. He explains something in Arabic. She pulls her head back and in a few minutes, a man's head appears. The guide explains again as the shopkeeper gives us an appraising look. He disappears and in ten minutes or so, the woman opens the door of the first floor shop. She can't find the lights.

The shop smells musty and is so dark I cannot see. It has the dank feel of a cave. Fans begin to revolve and now the shop smells of the spices this island is known for. In a few more minutes the owner appears, the lights are turned on and the richness of our adventure unfolds before our eyes. There are bright stacks of colorful books from floor to ceiling all around the room on shelves and on a central table. There are great piles of new books on the floor. Three of them we already own—*Maasai, African Elegance,* and *Wildest Africa.*

I ask the Arab owner for help finding just the right volumes on Zanzibar. The man explains that his son is a professional photographer and has contributed work to several of the books he has for sale. I choose three. We buy African folk tales about how the lion got his mane and the hippo got his smooth skin. We buy a beautiful coffee table book of Zanzibar photos that is the son's work. The third little book is about the architecture of Zanzibar and traces the history of the Swahili, Arab and Portuguese influences. We linger, looking at the antique Arab jewelry in a glass case. Cloves, cinnamon, coffee and nutmeg add spiciness to the moving air.

Janet, John and Pete visit the nearby stalls, photograph the children, buy spices and wait patiently. As I am about to check out, the man asks if we would like to see his home. I agree eagerly. Pete is less excited about the proposal, but willing, as are the Herrigels. Mr. Jefferji leads us to the back of the building through a tunnel, into a ramshackle courtyard and up a rickety set of wooden steps to the second floor. (Where is the Rotterdam? Do four American tourists disappear in the warrens of the Arab quarter of Zanzibar?)

On the next floor there is a large airy white walled room in the center of the building, open to the breezes and furnished with oriental carpets, hanging plants, beds and colorful pillows. It is easy to imagine languid Arabian nights in this environment. Wooden balconies on the third floor overhang the open space. There are several women skittering around in the side rooms, angrily eyeing us from a distance. We admire the room and ask polite questions, take some pictures and make our way back down the stairs. I keep urging Pete to get everything on video so we can look at it later. I find photographs of the very room we saw in the book on architecture. Evidently the son used his family home as an illustration of the interior of a typical house. What a terrific afternoon! You can trust an Arab.

We decide our afternoon has been such a success that we go right back to the ship. Waiting on the stone jetty, the heat, humidity, smells and congestion overwhelm us quickly. A woman passenger falls on the dock and bleeds profusely from a gash on her leg, dripping dark shiny puddles on the concrete. Her skin seems to be sensitive because the color of her leg is not normal. She is helped to the tender by the security officer. Another woman, we hear later, had her leg crushed between the tender and the docking platform when she missed the leap from tender to ship. It is difficult for some of the elderly ones to keep as much focus on the job they are doing as they need to have.

Pete and I entertain Table M for "sail away" cocktails in our cabin at six o'clock. There is relief when we all get back to the ship safely. We compare impressions of Zanzibar and tell jokes as the ship departs. The sky darkens, shore lights come on and an enormous full moon rises like a great apparition over the low dark hills of Zanzibar. It is a sight I will not forget.

KENYA—MOMBASA

FEBRUARY 20TH Sometimes my head can be full of romantic nonsense. This proves true about Kenya. We had a wonderful visit here four years ago and I have been anticipating a repeat. In the interval between trips *Out of Africa* has been one of my favorite books. I watch the film and reread bits of the book, savoring the arrangement of the words and the leisurely pace of Isak Dinesen's writing.

Today we dock in Mombasa with plans to drive by minivan on an overnight safari to Taita Hills, near Tsavo Park. We learn there will be a half-hour bumpy ride at first and then an additional two-hour drive to get to the game reserve.

Our dismay at the reality of the situation slowly grows. The trip takes five hours. The road surface is gone for half the distance, washed away two years ago in the La Nina flooding. Now we find it six inches deep in powdery red dust. The van bumps and slides over the rough road. We pitch to the right, then hard left. We careen and clatter over endless holes. Clouds of dust clog eyes, noses, ears, cameras. The windows are open and when a heavy lorry charges by, the red dust chokes us. We hang on and brace ourselves.

Lyle and Ev Reiswig, from Calgary, Canada, sitting on the back seat, bounce up high enough to hit the roof. Pete is in the front seat and Charlotte and Tim Nault and I are in the mid seats. Charlotte has asthma. We are concerned about her ability to handle such a dust storm but she seems to be enjoying herself. Tim rolls his big blue eyes at her and calls her "Mother" and is clearly worried about her. We have talked them into coming along and feel partly responsible for the unexpectedly miserable conditions of the ride.

When we arrive at Taita Hills, we are exhausted, filthy and I am angry. It has taken me a year and a half to get my spine back in shape after a ride on board seats in the back of a pickup truck in the Cape Verde Islands two years ago. I would never have come today if I had known what really was in store.

Our hotel room turns out to be at the top of the building, fifty long steps up from the lobby. No elevator, of course. Pete makes the trip up once and then just remains at ground level until the last trip up at night.

Our three-hour afternoon game drive is pleasant by comparison with the ride out. Right away we see seven leisurely lions lounging in the shade by a pond. The big male has a black mane. Several three-hundred-pound females loll contentedly nearby. One teenage lioness is feeling playful. She scratches the tree, leaps around the napping tawny shapes of her family, jumps to the top of a stump in the pond, with all four paws gathered for balance and then leaps to another stump. She tries like any teenager to interest others in her play, but the adults ignore her hijinks. We watch from a distance of a hundred yards for half-an-hour in the afternoon heat. Driving on, we see wildebeest, water buck, gazelles, antelopes, impala, dikdik, ostriches and herds of baboons.

The driver spots a grey shape moving through the greenery and then another and another. We pull to one side of the road and watch quietly as a herd of elephants move along a path toward a water hole. There are large tusked males and little two-year-olds, mid-size and large females and then more. As we sit, excited at our good luck, eighteen elephants saunter along, one after another, on their measured way. For a moment a massive bull turns in our direction and stops, watching us, flapping his enormous ears. He is satisfied and turns to go on with the family. We drive parallel to the path farther down the road and see the proud procession pass another open place in the bush. What a gift to see these extraordinary animals in their native surroundings! They are so much more dignified and at ease here than the ones we see at home in chains.

In the latter part of the afternoon we search for giraffes, but there are none. Our return to the lodge and the fifty stair climb to our second-floor room is the end of an exhausting day. We shower and change to fresh clothes and go down to the bar for a half hour before dinner. Gin and tonic with lime seems the right drink for this former British colony. It settles the dust of the day and revives us. The food and a little Maasai music from three shiny-skinned black warriors send us quickly off to bed. During the night, I hear mice chewing on some cracker crumbs I dropped on the floor. In the morning they are gone and a couple of teeth holes have been made in a granola bar in my back pack. The mosquito netting around the bed made me feel safe enough, even from mice.

Charlotte and Tim are thrilled with what we have seen. She is still hoping to see a giraffe. Her cheery attitude and excitement at being here are a tonic to all of us. She seems to be doing well enough as far as her allergies are concerned.

* * * * *

The next morning after an early breakfast we start out again. There are frequent sightings of various antelopes and baboons. Driving in the Land Rover over the deserted plains, our heads turn this way and that, searching for game. As we return to the road near Salt Lick Lodge, thirty zebra come, a few at a time, to cross the road right in front of us. Skittish young zebras with brown instead of black stripes cavort across the road, taking three steps for every one an adult takes. Again the giraffes are nowhere to be seen. But Charlotte and Tim make satisfied comments that tell us they are happy.

The road back to Mombasa is just as bad as the day before. It is made worse by our Indian driver's blaring horn. His contempt for the blacks walking along the edge of the road is obvious to us. He scatters mothers with small children, slow old people, men wheeling bicycles burdened with loads and young people walking to work. One man frowns a malevolent scowl at us. The driver disregards our requests to slow down and drive more carefully. Eventually we all just give up, hang on and pray for the trip to end safely. He had been fairly friendly on the trip out but now he is like a maniac, nonresponsive and with only one speed—too fast.

When Pete and I compare notes, we decide we have no desire to return to the interior of Kenya unless we fly. Masaii Mara is declared a wonderful trip by the Herrigals. Their plane flight made all the difference. They enjoyed every bit of it, but of course, it was two and a half times the price we paid at $1000 each.

Kenya used to be in good shape two decades ago, with decent roads and a calm population. Now roads are in ruins, the telephones barely work and the education system is collapsing. Foreign investors have disappeared. The focus of their displeasure is the dictatorial regime of President Daniel arap Moi. Tribal violence is being resurrected as the tourism industry disintegrates. Kenya is a country that is closed and just doesn't know it yet. My illusions are gone.

SEYCHELLES—VICTORIA

FEBRUARY 24TH The Seychelles have lingered in Pete's mind from four years ago as the place he liked the most on that earlier trip. Victoria on Mahe´ Island is a typical colonial town with clocks and statues, a Barclay's Bank and winding streets. We take the coast road out of town with Moe and Sylvia, heading by taxi for Beau Vallon Beach Hotel.

Along the shore road the driver stops at an attractive stone house under shady trees. Kreofleurage perfumes are made here. He wants us to experience perfume made of local spices: cinnamon, ylang ylang, vitiver, patchouli, vanilla, nutmeg and takamaka. It smells spicy and exotic. The bottle is installed in a wooden block with a peephole so the customer can tell how full it is and it is wrapped and tied with raffia. The package is a delight and so is the fragrance. At $30 for eleven milliliters, it seems expensive but unique. The company can be contacted on the web at www.dag@seychelles.net.

Our ride continues along the shore and suddenly the beauty of the day intrigues me. The sea is turquoise with white breakers, the beach is wide white sand and when we arrive at the hotel, it is open on all sides to the sea. As we settle contentedly into the chintz cushions of lobby sofas to enjoy a few moments of quiet, familiar American voices are heard. Here come Leslie and Tom from Cruise Specialists, with Dorey and Betty, Mary Ellen Hanley, John Stratton and others following. When a ship arrives at a small place, there are only so many sights to see. We all tend to congregate in what we hope will be an out-of-the-way place. We head back to town after buying T shirts for Ann and Bob Beck to thank them for caring for our dog part of the time.

SEYCHELLES—PRASLIN

FEBRUARY 25TH As Louis Pasteur said, "Chance favors the prepared mind." I took a class in sculpture once. That class gives me educated eyes when I look at the sea this morning. We are anchored off La Digue and Praslin Islands in the Seychelles group in the Indian Ocean, about four degrees south of the Equator. It is hot on the balcony just as the sun comes up.

Sculpture is about shape, size, materials and the texture of surfaces. Texture is accomplished by the process called "patination," a word with its roots in "patina." This morning the patina of the sea is the charm of it. Any sculptor would work long hours to accomplish such an intricate surface. It is a flat calm day and the smallest marks are cross-hatching. Next in size are concentric circles spreading out from the ship. Next larger in scale is dappling like little puffs all over the surface. Next larger are billows like sheep on a field, one after the other. There is a fifth pattern, invisible to my eyes, that makes a long slow swell so that the ship has a leisurely rock. It makes my stomach cry, "Breakfast, where is breakfast?"

It is six thirty AM. We go ashore at eight on a ship's shore excursion to Praslin. This is a brand new port for us, low lying islands not far from yesterday's port of Victoria, Mahe´, Seychelles. And, as if by magic, unlike a piece of sculpture, the surface of the sea changes as the sun comes up full. The surface pattern is altered and gone as busy ship's tenders churn the water, preparing to haul eight hundred of us ashore, a hundred at a time. The tranquillity that we came here to find is changed by the single fact that we are here. The art is to find a fragment of the locale in the brief time given to us where the surface remains the same in spite of our presence.

Praslin is one of only two islands where the giant palm, the cocoa de mer, grows. It measures 120 feet at forty years of age, matures to set seeds at that age and can live to be between two and four hundred years old. The fronds are enormous—as wide as a swimming pool, but the seeds are what the tree is most famous for. They are dark brown, double sided, look like a plump woman's backside and can weigh up to forty pounds. The seeds float far and wide on the Indian Ocean but none ever take root anywhere but here.

The bus takes us to the valley where the coco de mer grows. The rest of the tour group follows the guide on a path into the jungle. Pete and I return to a shelter with benches and wait in the quiet, listening to the birds singing. A little animal comes out of the woods, roots around in the leaves with its long pointed snout and poses for pictures, a tenrec. We feel we have had a special treat when the rest of the group returns, sweating and tired.

Our bus trip to the valley of the cocoa de mer ends with an hour at a beach. Granite rocks tumbled near shore and a white sand strip edging broad blue water make a vacationer's paradise. We have a beer at a beachfront bar while lots of Rotterdam passengers swim in the ocean. Fred, the printer from New York city and Judy, his slightly handicapped wife, join us at the table. She is a tall thin woman with a slight limp and a gung ho spirit. She makes sure she gets a swim while we lazy ones sit and watch.

There is a gift shop down the road. I find cards of buttons made of coconut shell sliced into various shapes. No two buttons on the card are the same, but they are all the same color. They will make an interesting addition to a dress. I also buy a string of blue coral beads which look like they are made out of some artificial substance and then shellacked. They are a gorgeous color. Everything here is expensive. We find that every place that has a French connection is always expensive.

MALDIVES—MALÉ

FEBRUARY 28ᵀᴴ The Maldive Islands are scattered like a string of lily pads across the Arabian sea southwest of India. None of these coral atolls lies more than six feet above sea level. We are visiting Male´, both a town and an island that is a half mile wide and a half mile long. Perhaps one reason for the stop is the fact that India won't accept travelers from yellow fever-infested countries within six days of their visit there. Our stop at Male´ gives us one day to spare before we sail to Cochin tomorrow. In order to visit many third-world places, we need shots and pills. Yellow fever, polio, and malaria are the chief concerns. Our local health department keeps us up to date. To the required immunizations, we add pneumonia, the current flu blend and hepatitis.

We are exposed to infections by traveling in these countries. Also every new group of passengers brings the current crop of germs from the United States on board the ship. On this trip we are using antibacterial hand soap to see if it cuts down on our sick days.

These islands are tiny. A three-story building under construction looks like it will upset the equilibrium of the pad it floats on. Visible over the buildings, the tail of a jet plane is higher than anything else on the island. The foundations of the buildings must tremble when a plane lands or takes off. We are here for just seven hours, from seven to two, so it's a stop just to say we've been here.

It turns out seven hours is more than enough. We take the tender to shore, arriving in heat and humidity, to find eager Indian men surround us as soon as we step ashore. One man decides we should take his taxi for $15 for an hour. Wherever would we go on such a tiny island? There are shills on the narrow sidewalk, saying "Come in my store—only the best prices!" We escape the crowd into a tiny shop where we buy boxes of silver with stones inset into the lids, postcards and a T-shirt of a particular pink I like. Some of their coral and silver necklaces are pretty but about a hundred dollars each. Our interest in the necklaces takes us to a different level of sales person. Rather than just buying what we want, we are invited to the dark recesses at the back of the store to bargain with the owner. We sit at the table with the Indian shopkeeper for fifteen minutes as the process develops. Once we sit down, more stuff is displayed for us in such rapid succession that we are overwhelmed. They really get aggressive as we start to squirm. Soon all we can think of is to get our boxes and get out of there.

When we leave the shop, fleas descend, along with heat, sewage smells, and the filthy narrow streets. The men pester and beg, reaching hands out to stop us. We run into Moe and Sylvia on the narrow crowded sidewalk. He is traveling in his black shorts and shirt with a big white bath towel around his neck, overheated and sweating. Enough of this. We head back to the dock.

Pete takes a video of the variety and confusion of the boats in the harbor—all shapes and sizes. A couple of dark-skinned men come to shore, climb high onto the stone dock from their outboard boat and reveal that they wear nothing else under their short bunched skirts.

The commotion of our tender landing has attracted a sweet faced Indian man in his forties. He is sitting on his homemade bicycle made from a high front wheel, a low back wheel, a hand crank with vertical chain drive, a seat, a basket and a collection of bits of wire and metal all strung together. He wears filthy rags draped over the stump where his right leg should be. He smiles when I ask if we may take his picture for that is his purpose in being there. We pay for taking the photo with a few dollars and get a fine smile of gratitude.

Here is the unreality of life. At lunch in the dining room on the ship in the clean, air-conditioned setting with a waiter tend-ing to every request, the contrast is overwhelming. Pete spends an hour talking stock trades with John Herrigel and Frank Matthews. Frank's wife, Tommie, and Janet and I make up the six-some. I hope that the beggar on the homemade bicycle at least has a good meal tonight and can afford a day or two of food. Why didn't we give him more?

INDIA—COCHIN

FEBRUARY 29TH The red brown roofs of Cochin are ranged in rows between luxuriant dark green palm trees. We sail up river in the early morning mist. Fishermen are busy at their huge square Chinese fish nets that line the river near the sea. Coconut palms are everywhere, their dense green fronds a solid mass above the buildings. The flat coastal area and many small waterways helped Cochin become the chief seaport on the west coast of India. For five hundred years European ships and great Arab dhows have carried pepper, cloves, nutmeg, coffee, and slaves to the Swahili coast of Africa and to western Europe.

The temperature is in the nineties. We climb carefully on a decrepit boat for a ride in full sun across an arm of the sea to Jewtown. Crumbling stairs, bathroom smells and climbing temperatures assault us at the landing. The weary old buildings look hundreds of years old, yellowing and mildewed. We walk narrow crowded streets, quickly wearying of our urge to see India. Insistent sellers of fans, necklaces and trinkets and the fetid heat combine to make our walk unpleasant.

We visit Matancherry Palace but don't go inside. Our decision to wait in the courtyard turns into an hour at the mercy of crowds of beggars and sellers. Every deformed person Pete sees elicits an instant response from him that they must have had polio. Several of us try to persuade him that parents deliberately deform their own children to make beggars of them. One man's pelvis has been broken so that his atrophied legs stick out sideways from his hips. His knees are forever at right angles to his thighs. He walks on his hands, where he wears sandals, dragging his useless legs along beneath him. His shape is that of a back-to-back letter "h."

When we return to the bus, I sink into the seat next to the window, grateful for the tiny fan that stirs the air. When I open my eyes after a few moments, there is a man right outside my window. He has met a pot of scalding water or oil that has burned him so terribly that his lips run down his face in a red ugly smear. His chest, shoulder and arm are a network of stiffened scar ridges. His face is twelve inches outside my bus window. My stomach churns to look at him so I shut my eyes. Every time I open them, he is still there, like a recurrent nightmare. Another fellow has a withered leg that is four inches shorter than his normal leg. We wait an hour for the others to return, besieged by these pathetic people. What difference in their lives would my few dollars make?

The heat, humidity, smells, open sewers, filth and relentless assaults of the beggars make me give up. I want to go away from here. There is no excitement, no sense of adventure left. I want to go back to sea air, a clean bed and decent food and leave all this far behind. India overwhelms my senses. India is depressing. So much poverty and filth, the crowds of insistent people, the dreary buildings, honking horns and the horrific beggars are more than I can take.

* * * * *

We had an incident at sea night before last when suddenly the ship listed hard. Bottles slid. Pete's walking stick by the cabin door fell. The ship creaked. We learned next morning that one of the propeller bearings malfunctioned. Yesterday Rotterdam was hot everywhere, especially in the dining room. We were a couple of hours late into port today and we were only to be here eight hours to start with. She was designed to cruise at twenty-five knots and has trouble keeping that speed. Our cabin air-conditioning is unreliable and has been since Capetown. Lucky we have the balcony and can keep our door open.

INDIA—MADRAS

MARCH 2ND The Rotterdam proceeds calmly up the channel into Madras, past the Hyundai plant, past lines of cranes and container ships, a tumbled stone seawall. All is quiet. Only slight ripples in the water and the slow progression of the scenery tell of our forward motion. The pilot boat accompanies us up the ever more industrial waterway, through a second breakwall. We pass dry docks and warehouses, and ships from all over the world. Rotterdam makes a hard starboard turn, using her thrusters which can almost turn us on a dime, our mighty horn bellows and we head for a dock lined with buses and waiting people. I can never appreciate the size of this great ship until she is in relation to things on land. Suddenly she feels gigantic. We stir huge boils of bottom sediment as we work our way slowly to the dock.

Madras was the seat of the British Empire for more than a hundred years—a great center for the manufacture of cotton cloth and typical plaid cotton fabric of the same name. The water is littered with garbage. Sounds of Indian drums and horns reach out to greet us. After our experience in Cochin two days ago, I am very reluctant to even go ashore today.

Sixteen officials come on board to clear the ship—a job normally handled by two or three. Someone said the main gift of the British to the Indians is bureaucracy and the Indians have expanded that gift. There must be a hundred men in white shirts and ties, milling around near rows of buses. The noise, dust, and confusion make a dock area that is intimidating. We walk the length of the dock, looking for a taxi. There isn't one in sight. It is impossible to tell how far we will have to go to find one.

When we round the terminal building, we are thrown into a maelstrom. Walking out of the fenced port compound, we are forced by walls and a locked gate to a railroad crossing where we wait for two trains to pass. Then we are corralled by stone walls into a one-man passageway, through a turnstile into a mob of men, pressing close against each other and us. We had been told to leave our video camera on the ship. Now we are happy we did.

Underfoot the way is broken and uneven; it is hard to walk, hard to keep our balance. Dust is deep. Wherever there is a puddle, I wonder what has just happened. We are grateful for solid leather shoes that can be wiped clean when we return to the ship. Everyone pulls at us, shouts at us, gets in our way, tries to get us to ride in their pedicab. Pete and I plough through the crowd to find an even worse situation at the edge of the street. Six lanes of horn honking congestion converge on us from both directions, with no idea of stopping for pedestrians. There are no crosswalks, no stoplights.

We look up and down the thoroughfare and hesitantly step out into the madness. We cross to the other side, breathless, and find ourselves no better off than before, except we are in the center of a group of sweet-smelling Indonesians from the ship.

As we realize there are no taxi stands and the traffic never slows down, a little man runs up to us. "I have a cab, madam," he says in a sing-song voice. He points across the road. We agree to have him drive us and he brings a white jitney around through the traffic to our side of the street. As we settle on the broken springs of the back seat, we realize he is just a shill. Another man who speaks no English is driving. We tell the guide to take us to the Connemara Hotel and hang on as the cab hurtles through the traffic, horn blaring. Car horns here are both a defensive and aggressive weapon.

The shill talks on and on, trying to get us to agree to go shopping, pointing out weary red brick buildings left from the days of the British empire. The noise, confusion, density of people and traffic, the dirt, dust, old posters, crumbling walks, shacks along the sides of the streets, animals, children and women in filthy saris remind me of an overfilled charm bracelet where each symbol is packed tight against the next. The paintings of Pieter Breughel come to mind. Each person is pursuing his own life, from the naked children to the old woman standing in the gutter next to the traffic with a wet puddle spreading below the hem of her worn red sari.

We reach the gated enclosure of the old British hotel with relief and overpay the taxi to get rid of them. The restaurant gives us a quiet corner to sit and regroup. If the ship had come in on time, we had planned to eat an Indian lunch here but due to the circumstances and the hour, we settle for Kingfisher beer, coffee and some chili cheese toast. Our bill comes to six dollars. Pete leaves a ten. He is told later that tipping is not done—it is considered improper.

The tall elegant doorman dressed in white with a commanding turban and a crimson sash finds another cab for us, gives the driver the location of the ship and tells us the price. For one half what we paid coming, we return to the port. The only way to get into the dock area is back through the crowd, through the turnstile under the eyes of the police, back across train tracks, over potholes, around the building and up the gangplank. We have seen something of Madras and have been overwhelmed in every dimension. When we get back to the cabin, before entering, we take off our shoes and wash them.

1. Our ship, the Rotterdam, flagship of Holland America Line.

2. The Inca ruins at Tambo Colorado near General San Martin, Peru.

3. The iron street sign at Frutillar, near Lake Llanquihue. Osorno volcano is across the lake.

4. Pete talking on Moe's Iridium phone in Antarctica.

5. Houseboats line the Grand Canal in Wuxi, China.

6. The garden of a Samurai house echoes the contours of the distant mountains.

7. A temple's elegant roofline improves on nature.

8. Costa Rican actors at Café Britt make coffee farming funny.

9. Engineers use terracing to stabilize a cut through mountains at the Panama Canal.

10. Table M—from the left: Pete and Betty Anne Reininga, Peggy Masica, Tim Nault, Gene Masica, Lynn Anderson, Charlotte Nault, Chuck Anderson, Moe and Sylvia Craddock at lunch in the La Fontaine Dining Room.

THAILAND—PHUKET

MARCH 5TH The ship is sailing in the early morning from the Andaman Sea to the southern coast of Thailand. Grey island shapes are scattered like clouds in the sky. Rose and grey streaks hint at the new day. We hope to dock instead of having to tender in to Phuket. Docking is tricky, according to yesterday's Voice from the Bridge. Since the Rotterdam is forty feet too long for the available space, clearance from the harbormaster is required. In the most ideal conditions and with special permission, Captain Dijk will back this huge ship to the dock. Not only does the weather have to be perfect as we arrive, but it has to remain perfect for the twelve hours we are in port. Being right next to the dock is of crucial importance for this is where the flea market to end all flea markets usually occurs.

Phuket is a famous vacation area, known since the 1970's for its beaches, scenery, golf, scuba, snorkeling and wonderful Thai food. Part of the James Bond movie, *Tomorrow Never Dies*, was filmed here in this dramatic scenery. We slide smoothly in to dock at the little pier. Souvenir stalls haven't been set up yet, but they will be here when we return tonight.

A bus takes us to Lighthouse Point overlooking a calm blue bay. Up near the top of the long hill is a gold-turreted spirit-house surrounded by a concrete plaza, ringed with a double row of carved wooden elephants. Each elephant represents a prayer answered, according to the tour guide. She says that if your wish comes true, you take an offering elephant to the god in the shrine and add it to the circle. The hundreds of elephants in the circle tell us this god is very powerful. Other offerings in this Buddhist country include yards of colorful fabric tied around old trees—offerings to the spirits that live in the trees. The fabric strips blowing in the wind seem to be prayers winging their way to heaven. The fabric will protect these old trees from being cut down.

At the next stop we hop down from our double-deck bus. These are familiar surroundings, the same gift shop, Wang Talang on Vichitsongkram Road, that we visited four years ago. I sort through all the ready made silk garments that are either too small for me or unattractive colors. Since I am blonde and fair skinned, I find colors are not complimentary to me when we are in a country where the people have dark skins. A sudden inspiration takes me to the display of row on row of softly gleaming silks. In a few minutes I buy five yards of dark blue-green silk with the idea of having it made up by a tailor in Hong Kong. At $20 a yard, I hope it is good quality silk.

Lunch is at the 4000 seat Thai Naan restaurant just across the street. Every dish is labeled. Some are familiar, some not. There are sweet-and-sour dishes, curried chicken, cashew chicken; some of them are hotter than we are used to. There is a tiny bowl of bright green and red miniature peppers in a clear liquid (vinegar?) with round red balls and black bits and seeds. I guess right that this relish will add heat to other dishes. Pete bravely tries a fair-sized bite all by itself and suddenly he is grasping water and beer and other food and fruit, trying to find something to quiet the burn. For dessert we eat steamed bananas in warm sweetened coconut milk. They are unusual and tasty after the spicy food.

An afternoon cultural show sends us to an amphitheater for Thai dancing, kick-boxing and musicians. Later we go out back of the building to an arena for an elephant show. In Thailand the logging industry has been regulated out of existence, so owners are looking for useful ways to employ their elephant friends. Giving rides after the show is one of the answers. All goes smoothly until one passenger, a large woman, somehow slips between the elephant and the platform used to board the beast. She is injured, and is taken to a hospital and then flown directly back to the United States. Some said she broke her hip, but no-one seems sure quite what happened. All things considered however, Thailand is a welcome relief after India.

The market on the dock is in business when we return to the ship. We come back tired and it is hot outside, so we eat dinner and then go down to the line of shops. Katerina tells us she bought all kinds of logo carryalls and we go down looking for the same space. Before long I buy a Louis Vuitton purse for Kathy and another for myself. Her's is traditional brown leather with wonderful heavy gold hardware. Mine is a silver bucket bag. The salesman demonstrates that both are real leather by holding his lit cigarette lighter right next to the surface of the bag. It does no damage. The bags are $35 each, a real bargain if they are genuine.

* * * * *

One night, the opened curtains reveal a hundred or more tiny lights riding low on a silent sea. Lights in sets of three shine across the water, some close to the ship's path, others farther away. They twinkle in a long line on our starboard side, as far as I can see. They must be little fishing boats and each must have his lights on to attract fish to his nets. It is a magical sight, like fairies dancing in a dark wood. Mundane matters require me to get up sometimes at three-thirty in the morning—for a cracker to calm the tummy, an aspirin for an aching foot, a wish to know the time, for we have an early tour. I always check the view before returning to bed. The unexpected sight of the fishing boats gives me a vision to take happily back to dream on. I have read about the cuttlefish fleets. Is this what I saw?

SINGAPORE

MARCH 7TH We are eager to get off the ship as fast as we can this morning. The Masicas, the Andersons, Pete and I plan to go to the Singapore Zoo for breakfast with the orangutans. Several taxis take us for a forty minute ride across the city. There we buy tickets for breakfast and ride a trolley through the landscaped garden to the orang pavilion half way around the track. We arrive on time—a real accomplishment, for the ship was cleared at eight and we made it here by nine. Breakfast is quickly over. A mama orangutan and her small baby are led to a seat near a high table under the trees. Fruit is spread in front of the animals. As they eat durian and bananas, each of us has a chance to have a picture taken with them.

We also visit the Komodo dragon, the white rhinos and the monkey show and later get a ringside seat for an elephant show. The trolley, the gardens and the clean conditions make for an enjoyable morning. Lynn Anderson buys a new special purse similar to one Peggy has at the gift shop. We get back to the ship, pleased with ourselves, by noon. Joann and Bill Blackburn from Oldsmar arrive today for three weeks to Osaka, Japan. They bring welcome news of home and friends.

* * * * *

The next day at sea, March 8th, the ship holds a "Man Overboard" drill. In the middle of the day, unannounced, a dummy in a bright orange life jacket is thrown over a rail. Bells ring, an announcement is made, the ship executes a full Williamson turn and we retrace our path to the spot where the dummy was tossed. A tender is launched and the crew mans her, as they putt to the spot. We are all happy that it was not a real person, for it took forty-five minutes to retrieve the dummy. The Captain promises another drill soon in order to improve the crew's time.

VIETNAM—VUNG TAU

MARCH 9TH When it rains, it rains hot water here. This lush jungle and swamp is famous for the miserable conditions US soldiers faced during the war in the sixties. Luckily, we have no rain today and since it is March, the temperatures are as cool as they can get. The ship sails into Vung Tau on the Mekong delta. We found Vietnam a fascinating place when we first visited four years ago in Da Nang and Hue. Memories of war and haunting scenes on nightly television were softened by the reality of 1996. We wonder what new impressions will be added today.

A group of dragon dancers greets us. Cymbals clang as the imaginary dragon leaps and weaves along the dock. At a rest stop, there is one beggar, a wizened old brown skinned woman, wrinkled and bent, who holds out her hand passively. We see lots of traffic in the cities: bicycles, motorbikes, buses, but little in between towns. People wear masks over their faces, against the dust of the streets. Conical hats tied under the chin decorate the pretty young women. The people seem purposeful and the shops look prosperous.

After the Presidential Palace and lunch at the Marriott Hotel, we visit the Vietnamese Folk Water Puppets, an art form originated in 1121. A pond surrounded by white plastic chairs has curtains along one side. Odd stiff figures of men with baskets try to catch the fish that cavort and splash. Six demure women puppets with stark white faces and graceful hands do a little dance. Music plays as we watch, entranced. The puppets are manipulated by long poles underwater, from behind the curtain. At the end four men wade out in waist deep water, clasp their hands chest high and bow low.

I have been looking today for the Vietnam of the Catherine De Neuve film, *Indochine*—the rain, the islands, the superstitions. Instead we see a dynamic country moving forward, searching for economic stability. We read about the absence of civil rights but you can't see that problem just driving through.

* * * * *

Bill Blackburn, Charlotte Nault and I find a way to enjoy our favorite ice cream, without the observant eyes of the whole dinner table. We go in the afternoon to the Lido for a banana split. Using a salad plate gives us more room for our favorite dessert. The banana is just an excuse to eat all the other parts of the typical sundae: ice cream, nuts, sauces, whipped cream. We act like guilty school-children as we eat ice cream to our heart's content.

CHINA—HONG KONG

MARCH 10TH We need no sunglasses in Hong Kong. For one whole day and two part days, the clouds hang at the tops of the skyscrapers. Grey clouds, silver buildings and grey sea blend in a monotone scene except at night when the neon lights excite the sky. Fog, mist and rain diminish our activities.

Nothing stops the eager traveler except for our friend, Chuck Anderson. We return from shore and happen to have lunch with him. His merry eyes dart about and I can see how excited he is to be here. He needs his motorized wheelchair to get around and he cannot find a way to get it down into the big new Cruise Terminal. There are six or eight steps at every entrance and no elevators. He is resigned to staying on board and doing laundry. No-one who isn't in the same circumstances can understand the frustration when barriers to the physically challenged bar the way.

The city is even more crowded than when we were here four years ago. Our dock is right downtown in the middle of the towering skyscrapers of Tsimshatsui. Where we saw block after block of old concrete ten-story "factory" buildings last time, there are far fewer derelict buildings now. Glittering forty-story new skyscrapers of dramatic shape are everywhere. Apartment buildings that once had a view of the harbor are now behind all the new development.

Saturday night we go ashore with the Blackburns for a night on the town with Angela Wong of Abercrombie and Kent. She brings a twenty-passenger bus to carry us to the Lei Yue Mun fishing village for dinner. We don't pick out the living creatures to eat this visit as we did the last time we were here, but everything is alive until it is cooked for us.

Thousand year old eggs, black and gooey, begin the meal. The gelatinous quality and the black color makes them difficult to eat, but some of us persevere, determined to try everything. A slice of raw ginger in the same mouthful perks up the flavor. Platters appear every fifteen minutes—one with six-inch-long fried prawns, one with a green vegetable they call spinach. This vegetable is unlike what we know, with its stalks and leaves, but it is tasty. The deep fried prawns are delicious.

We look forward to a platter of scallops, but instead of the tiny tender ones we get at home, these are large muffin-size mollusks with a black fringe of inedible matter. They come between paper thin grayish-green flat shells. Not what we anticipated. The best dish of the evening to all four of us is the final one—whole grouper, deep fried to a delicate brown crispness. I often remove the skin from fish but even the skin of this fish is delicious. We eat the whole fish (it must have weighed five pounds) and praise it as the best grouper any of us have ever eaten. Even Florida grouper can't compare.

Fresh watermelon center slices make the perfect dessert. Angela asks if we like sweet potatoes. We should not have said yes, but when we do, a warm sweet soup comes as a second dessert. It has lumps floating in it, of sweet potato and sticky rice balls that have the texture of fish eyes. We should have stopped with the watermelon.

Hong Kong seems prosperous to our eyes, but Angela talks about the impact of the financial bump in Asian markets three years ago. Residents who bought apartments then have been subject to a devaluation of 50%. Their payments make them "upside down" in the value of their asset. She says the cost of an apartment now is $1000 US per square foot. That is a half million dollars for a 500 square foot apartment. Perhaps as many as ten members of a family will live in this size space, with one bathroom. There must be a lot of mutual respect and self-control in such crowded conditions. A low-income family pays $100 a month for a 10 by 30 space and will use screens to divide it. Other things are so expensive, I wonder how they manage.

* * * * *

Katerina, our animal-loving friend from Atlanta, tells me a horrifying experience that happened to her on her last visit to Hong Kong. She was a guest of honor at an elaborate dinner. When they arrived at the restaurant, they were seated at a round table for ten that had a hole in the center of the table. Chained in the hole was a live monkey. One of the courses of the dinner was the still warm brain of the recently alive monkey. She says she fled the room. She was sick in the bathroom and didn't return to the party.

Pets are popular, but not dogs or cats. (Have they all been eaten already?) Birds and fish are the pets of choice. Elderly men take their birds in cages to the park in the early mornings and give them an outing while they perform tai chi exercises.

* * * * *

I postponed my visit to a Hong Kong tailor so we could have our dinner last night. This morning, Sunday, I appear at the door of the British tailor shop next to the Hong Kong Hotel in the terminal at 10 AM. I take my purple silk evening dress to be copied in the peacock blue Thai silk from our stop in Phuket. They tell me clearly they cannot finish a dress in the twenty-seven hours remaining before we sail, but they say to come back Monday noon for a fitting. The shop will ship it when finished to Florida. I am disappointed but not surprised. I had hoped to have something almost green to wear for the St. Patrick's Day party we will host with Frank Clyne and Mary Ellen Hanley.

This afternoon I spent two hours tramping the corridors of the enormous Terminal mall, looking for a rubber stamp or confetti or stickers that symbolize St. Patrick's Day. I see Easter, Halloween, Christmas and children's animals and monsters, but no Irish stuff. There cannot be any Irish living here. Finally, in a last desperate search for something to add a touch of festivity to our party invitations, I find, on my third pass down the stamp rack at Toys R Us, a four leaf clover mini-stamp in green that will do. The invitations for St. Patrick's Day cocktails go out sprinkled with little green "shamrocks."

* * * * *

Monday morning I take a "deluxe shopping trip" offered by the Shore Excursion office. We first visit a jewelry factory where diamonds and gold are spectacular and the jade is amazing. It comes in brown, blue, lavender and white. They offer cases full of antique jade pieces. I look at everything quietly, avoiding the help of a salesperson. Pete and I have been talking about how soon we can take another world cruise. He says the timing depends on the "have-to-have list." I know that if I shop here, it will cost serious dollars so I keep my hands in my pockets.

Our next stop is the Wah Tung porcelain factory in the Grand Marine Industrial Building at 3 Yue Fung Street in Aberdeen: four floors of jugs, jars, platters, tureens, pots and animals. My resolve evaporates. I buy a platter called a "charger" decorated with aqua, blue and pink tobacco leaves and a little perky bird. It will replace a similar size platter in Florida that we broke and glued back together years ago. The black wood "ox-horn" stand it is displayed on is handsome, so I have one of those shipped home too.

I leave the tour before the bus gets to Stanley market for lunch in order to return for a fitting on my dress. A twelve dollar taxi ride and a twenty five cent Star Ferry ride will return me to the Ocean Terminal. Little tingles of apprehension go with me on the ferry ride. I don't often go off on my own in a huge city. I hug my purse close as we ride the short distance. The crowd of students, grandmas with little children, old women pulling carts and young businessmen disgorges into the green, austere ferry building. Suddenly I am back in the familiar part of the city. My apprehensions vanish.

The tailor has the dress made and lined with green silk. It even has self-covered buttons. I am dismayed at how big it is, but a man in the shop makes everything better by saying, "You look like a million dollars in that dress!" The tailor will move the buttons, shorten the sleeves, and take in the seams. I ask if it can be finished in two hours. I am delighted when they say "yes." I retrieve my prize at one o'clock. We sail at two.

* * * * *

It never occurred to me that I could lose a pair of pants on a cruise ship. When I pack, I try to be conservative about the amount of clothing I take, but somehow the suitcases always bulge. I have one pair of Tilley soft floppy pants with a zippered inside pocket for really hot days on shore. They rinse and drip dry. But I had two pairs when I started out. One lightweight navy pair of pants was easy to hand-wash. When I rinsed them out the first time, it seemed right to wrap them in a towel to get out the excess moisture. There they stayed. I forgot to take them out. The towels went down to the laundry and the pants were never seen again. I really miss those pants, especially since they had an elastic waist—a very accommodating feature.

When we pack for one hundred evenings of casual, informal and formal dress, we already have a generous number of outfits. But then throw daytime on-board clothes and daytime shore excursion gear into the mix. I take two pairs of Tilley Endurable twills for basic shore wear. I rarely wear shorts on shore, even in extreme heat. A skirt for shore is not included because when boarding tenders or crossing windy gangplanks, skirts can be trouble.

Evening clothes come first on the list. My solution, since I don't wear formal clothes at home, is four pairs of long pants with sweaters, shirts, a beaded jacket, and an assortment of scarves and stoles. I mix and match these with an old embroidered Chinese-silk piano scarf and a pashmina shawl. I have two formal long dresses for the most special events, like the Captain's dinner. For informal evenings when men wear jackets and ties, I take suits, jackets and dressy pants or skirts. During casual nights, matched sets of resort wear are in order.

There are so many extras that we have to find room for. We always take small flashlights since the time when the old Rotterdam lost power off Bali. A couple of alarm clocks are necessary, for Holland America does not provide a clock in the cabin. There is a hairdryer in every bathroom, however. Shampoo and soap are stocked in the bathroom and other cosmetics are available at the shops on board. Toothpaste and similar products can be bought in the shop. Liquor is for sale in the shops at reasonable cost. Wine is sold at the per-glass price times the number of drinks in the bottle, so it is expensive. Beauty shop and spa services are extensive but pricey. A perm costs me double what it would at home.

CHINA—SHANGHAI

MARCH 15TH The Yangtze river is one of the busiest on earth. Grey shapes emerge into clear focus and then drift slowly away, dissolving into the mist. Chinese gunboats and missile carriers cluster near the entrance to the river, protecting the underbelly of China from invaders. The channel is narrow. We can imagine the concern on the bridge. Tension must be thick. I can see the profiles of deck officers as they pace, watching from every angle as we move slowly through the mist. We sail up the Yangtze and across the bar into the Whangpo in thick early morning fog. Colors and shapes flatten out. The silence has an echo.

The cold is penetrating this morning. When the ship's staff switches to navy blue uniforms, we know cold weather is coming. They changed two days ago and passengers have gradually put away shorts and T shirts. Now we all wear sweaters and slacks or the warm fleece vests and bush hats Cruise Specialists gave us. It feels good to be bundled up against our return to early spring in the Northern Hemisphere.

Our bus shows us a new Shanghai. The guide speaks glowingly of the advantages of the Chinese Communist system. She gets tiresome as she brags about the standard of living, the new apartments being built and what a cosmopolitan city this is. We remember the river front street in Shanghai called the Bund from our last trip ten years ago and can see the changes. Numerous skyscrapers have been built on both sides of the river. They are examples of the policy of the present Chinese government of spending money on this city to make it competitive with Hong Kong.

The double bulbed central television tower is a landmark, like some huge exercise dumbbell against the sky. Forty and fifty story buildings in good modern design line the Bund. Old four story apartment buildings draped with clothes drying on balconies are few and far between now.

By bus we go to the new Shanghai Museum on People's Square, built in 1997. The beautiful building, with terrazzo floors, displays handsome Chinese furniture, jade collections, calligraphy and paintings. We see an overview of China's artistic history since 5000 BC. In the shop I buy a hand-painted silk T-shaped dress for $60 that will make a formal outfit with my turquoise palazzo pants. I also get a sweatshirt that has been cut up the front and appliquéd with letters that spell out Shanghai Museum on the front, up the sleeves and on the back. You have to turn this way and that to make sense of the letters.

Our next visit is to the Yuyuan Gardens, built in 1577. They are in the heart of the city, surrounded by high walls, with apartments looking down from all sides. There is a house with curved tile roofs and many tiny vistas of rocks, trees, water and winding paths. Hundreds of tourists tramp through the garden in the rain—over the high thresholds that keep the evil spirits out, through the circular arches, across the brick courtyards, past the flowering camellias. By the pond a weeping willow is showing the first green of spring. All I can think of is how lovely this place might be if you could have it to yourself. The paths are short, steps are low, the vistas and proportions beautiful. As we turn each corner, I wonder how many little bound women's feet used to flutter through these same passages. Such perfection of proportion can not be defeated by the press of the crowd. When a wild bird sings and we hear the cry of a peacock in the distance, it is easy to imagine how life might have been in this place.

* * * * *

A woman who lived four doors from us on Verandah deck is found dead this morning. Suko, the cabin steward, carried breakfast to her, to find that she couldn't be roused. Suddenly real life intrudes into our idyllic existence. She was removed from her cabin unobtrusively and taken down to one of the large coolers where they probably had to move fresh flowers aside to make room for her. If arrangements can be made, the body will be shipped home from China. If not, we carry her along on the rest of the cruise until cooperative authorities can be found. A final note of farewell is the removal of the penguin from her door. Our hallway is more quiet than ever. We pull her invitation to the St. Patrick's Day party. Someone says she has had heart problems for years and that she was probably happier leaving from here than she would have been dying at home, watching television. The intrusion of reality into this wonderful voyage sobers our thoughts.

CHINA—XINGANG

March 16th With ship-shaking vibration and tremendous noise from powerful engines, the "pilot" boat pulls alongside. A dozen green-suited Chinese army officials board our ship, along with the harbor pilot, who is dressed in a long grey topcoat. As the huge rubber ringed tug rumbles by the starboard hatch, waiting for the men to transfer to the ship, our verandah floor vibrates and rattles. The awesome noise and power of the boat reminds me of the sound of an enormous army tank as it grinds up city streets.

We find that room service for breakfast is a great idea when there is an early morning shore excursion. It is delivered as early as 6:30 and arrives hot, fresh, well-toasted as circumstances require. Ham and cheese omelets from the room service kitchen are better than they are in the dining room. Toasted English muffins are heated to brown crispness unlike the warm muffins we sometimes get in the dining room.

The day in Wuxi by train is a challenge. We transfer by bus to a crowded train station and have to walk fast across a plaza, through the station to the Soft Seat Waiting Room. After a brief pause there, we walk through a hall, down two long flights of stairs, through a tunnel under the tracks and back up about fifty stairs. Pete can't keep up and we are far behind when the train comes into view. I alternate between concern that we will get lost and sympathy with how hard he is trying. When we reach the train, we still have a long walk down its length to car three. We sink with relief into the seats and enjoy the hour-and-fifteen minute ride to Wuxi.

Our group boards a colorful river boat for a short ride on the

Grand Canal. The edges are concrete lined with weeping willows softening the profile. We pass dozens of work boats where families live aboard. Women are busy hanging laundry and washing cooking pots. Little children wave and smile. One third of the canal near Beijing is unnavigable, the central third is usable only during the rainy season, and the third nearest Shanghai is used year round. The canal is 1100 miles long, was built in 500 BC. and is visible from space.

After a trip to a porcelain factory, there is a good Chinese ten-course lunch at the Wuxi Grand Hotel. In the afternoon we visit Ji Chang garden, four hundred years old, scenic, miniature and, again, overwhelmed with tourists. These gardens require four conditions to be classic—water, trees to symbolize the forest, rocks for mountains and a building of some sort from which to view it. When Pete and I lag behind, we have a few minutes to see the garden at peace. Suddenly Bill Blackburn comes back to get us and says we have to hurry because the group will leave by a different path. Another long walk gets us back to the bus.

Some things are noticeable by their absence. Nowhere today did we see any birds on the streets or in trees. Have they all been eaten? There are no dogs or cats. With such dense populations, large pets are not wanted in the cities. We are told that dog licenses are prohibitively expensive. A typical license fee is $1200 for the first year and $750 each year after. Dogs are not the only unwanted ones. As thick as the crowds are, we never see anyone in a wheelchair or on crutches. What has become of handicapped people in this country?

As we approach the train station, we are hopeful that this time we can escape the tunnel trip, but no, we have to repeat the fifty steps down, across and back up again. Pete, with his walking stick, camera around his neck and determination in the set of his jaw, gets help from a passing Chinese man, who literally hauls him up the steps on the other side. Back on the train again, my husband collapses and sleeps. We both know how much more walking lies ahead. By the time we get back to the ship, he is exhausted. Holland America designates the difficulty of each day trip with symbols of one man walking for an easy trip, up to three for a very difficult one. We will have to be more careful about the categories we choose from now on. This has been too hard on him.

There is a full moon tonight over the port yards of Xingang. What a far place from the beauty of the moon that night as we sailed from Zanzibar. Here the cranes keep working even after dark, moving steel bars, coils of wire and containers around the dock area. Storage compounds near the docks have long windrows of coal in orderly lines. There is smog from the coal fires in the city. Yesterday everyone who went to the Forbidden City in Beijing said that after they passed beyond Tianjin, they left the smog behind and the day was cold but beautiful. Smog and noise here seem perpetual.

* * * * *

We spend a cold spring day in Tianjin, the third largest city in modern China, the largest port city, home to ten million people. We stop first at the rebuilt old center city, and have to cross several lanes of traffic on a busy road. There are no pedestrian cross walks here. Taxis and bicycles whiz past as we dodge the thick traffic. Pete can't move that fast today. He says he has pain in his left shoulder, probably from the helpful Chinese who almost lifted him up the steps in the train station yesterday.

We buy toys for the children from sidewalk vendors in the narrow alleys of the old center city. A man waves a toy in front of us, something I remember having as a child: a thin wooden paddle carrying six pecking chickens. When we swing a ball around in circles under the paddle, the chickens take turns pecking corn. Two of them for the three-year-olds go with us, as do four finely made miniature steel racing bicycles with turning pedals, wheels and working hand brakes.

As we bargain with the lady selling the bicycles, a crowd of silent Chinese men gathers, listening and watching while the transaction develops. Maybe they are part of the sales force, for we feel uncomfortable as they watch and we bargain. The salesperson clearly wants to be satisfied. When we settle on $7 per bike, smiles break out on all the faces.

A young boy of about ten, dressed in yellow says to me, "Hello, how are you?" I reply in English and he tries more words, in a very formal and proper voice. The crowd smiles as we speak English. He is a beautiful child with well combed hair and nice clothes. Two older women are with him. Pete takes our picture as we repeat the very formal conversation and then shows it to him on the video camera. The boy and his relatives and the crowd are delighted to see their images on the screen. We shake hands and bow as we say goodbye. That is the second precious moment a young boy has given us this trip.

Along the street in the old city we meet Mary Lu and George Hendrie. He talks about being in Tianjin fifty-five years ago at the end of World War II. His ship was stationed here for a week while they had R and R. He remembers how poor the people were then and how little food there was. He says that every morning a cart would rumble through these streets, collecting the bodies of those who had died during the night.

Our shore excursion turns into a glorified shopping trip as we visit a carpet factory, a cloisonné shop and a wood block painting store. After watching the labor-intensive techniques, we think gift shop prices will be high. I buy two little heart-shaped fabric covered books with heart shaped pages and Happy New Year's paintings inside. They are inexpensive, colorful and exotic.

We drive past all the new skyscrapers but there are also slums with rotting roofs and a bare six feet between wandering rows of grey-brown buildings. The Chinese government has an amazing task, trying to provide homes and food for all these billions of people. The parched smog-filled atmosphere adds to the difficulty of living here. Pulmonary disease must be common to these scurrying people.

Pete is feeling more pain in his left shoulder as the long day advances. After a Chinese lunch at a local hotel, he stays on the bus, silent and trying to sleep. We can't get back to the ship fast enough for him.

* * * * *

On St. Patrick's Day Frank Clyne, Mary Ellen Hanley, Pete and I join forces to entertain two hundred of our friends for cocktails. The Crow's Nest is decked in balloons, streamers and banners with shamrocks everywhere. Frank makes arrangements for George Kowalski's band to play for the party. George has been a Holland America fixture for thirty-five years, previously in the Ambassador Lounge on the old Rotterdam and now in the Ocean Bar. George knows Frank can do an Irish Jig, so after the receiving line is over, he strikes up the music. Frank and Mary Ellen hold center stage with the flash bulbs popping, as they jump and hoof for the crowd. The hour passes quickly. We traipse in late for dinner, but filled with pleasure because things apparently went well. Giving a party is a tradition among many of the full cruise guests.

CHINA—DALIAN

MARCH 20TH The shore excursion brochure advertised a "home visit" so this morning we are climbing two flights of crumbling concrete steps in an apartment house to a multi-locked steel door. With smile-wreathed faces, two Chinese about our age welcome us into their apartment. We are led through a tiny entry into a little sitting room just long enough for two settees facing each other and a scrap of window at the end. Our hostess gestures to us to sit down. At the window end of the small room there is a tiny balcony with two birds in cages hung out in the cold morning sunshine. Our hostess passes overflowing bowls of peanuts in the shell and apples which are softer than they should be.

Suddenly in the doorway a cherub appears: a rosy-cheeked, bright-eyed little boy of three. Shy at first, he soon has us all smiling as he hands out one peanut at a time and then gravely puts the shells into a plastic container on a small table. One guest gives him a postcard of the ship, which he loves. Another gives him a piece of hard candy which he pops into his mouth.

We gravely sit on our hard seats when what we really want is to explore the small rooms. A few of us at a time circulate. We are led down a small hall to immaculately clean bedrooms, one with two little bicycles, past a wee interior kitchen with a four foot counter, a two-burner gas hot plate and no light to work by. There is a small but complete bathroom with tub, sink and toilet. In the little entry hall, next to the bathroom, there is a small two-door refrigerator. Apparently this room is also where the family eats.

The whole apartment is floored with linoleum and has whitewashed walls and lots of sunshine in the rooms that face front.

There is a television set and a small washing machine so they seem to be a fairly prosperous family. It is hard to determine how many other people live in this apartment, but we guess at least two more and maybe three. The space must be about five hundred square feet, tiny by our definition. We are told that the man of the family, a dignified gentleman, is a former railroad employee and this building for retired railroad workers is owned by their trade association. There is no elevator. The rent is higher on the ground floor and decreases as there are more stairs to climb.

Pete finds the building depressing and poorly maintained and is amazed that it is said to be only ten years old. As we leave we find that the pipes for water are above ground and ugly, running everywhere along the street.

Chinese hotel lunches are generous and delicious. Today we are greeted with a few plates of tidbits: boiled peanuts, dried bits of fish and shredded cabbage. There is a menu so we can track our way through ten platters of food that arrive. Spicy cashew chicken is followed by beef and pea pods, sweet and sour fried fish, a roasted chicken with head and feet still on, one or two green vegetables, spring onions sautéed with squid tentacles (delicious!), and more. Usually the meal ends with a generous bowl of steaming soup and a final platter of stir fried rice. Sometimes we are served watermelon. Beer or Coca Cola are the drinks of choice, usually in endless amounts.

I'm making a real effort to eat with chopsticks and can manage most of the meal. Yesterday we were presented with forks and knives. I think the chopsticks make me eat more slowly and eat less food, so I asked for them. I'm proud to be able to manage a boiled peanut with chopsticks.

As the day goes by, Pete is bothered increasingly by his left shoulder. When we return to the ship, I take him to the infirmary. After an EKG, the doctor compliments him on the good state of his heart, saying, "I'd be happy to trade for your test results. Your problem is muscle strain in your shoulder." Our thoughts flash back to the helpful Chinese man who practically lifted him up those fifty steps in Wuxi. He heads to bed with a fistful of pills and hope for quick relief.

* * * * *

We have a day at sea, which Pete spends in bed. He hauls himself out at lunch time to eat with Porter and Janet Reed. Lucky he did, for Porter raids his personal pharmacy and gives Pete hydrocodone. Finally he gets a pill which helps relieve the severe pain. He sleeps in comfort through the afternoon, uses the sauna and hot tub and even goes down to dinner. The Rifes and Wolfs give a cocktail party and he manages that too.

Nell Carter is the evening entertainer. She is a fat muffin on little short legs and she shakes and shimmies her huge weight in time with her singing. Her voice is obscured by the forceful band behind her. We both leave early, happy to go to bed.

* * * * *

Big Willem Regelink, the Chief Housekeeper, 6'6" of imposing height and girth, is a Dutchman who commands respect. He passes like a great white shark trailing a cloud of remora, followed by a cluster of white-suited worried looking Indonesians. We rarely see him on the cabin decks. He can rely on his carefully trained staff. The ship is clean, well maintained and there are no mice or varmints. He is gracious and a good person to know if you are careful not to ask for too much too often. Over the years he has arranged to get slacks hemmed in the tailor shop, have a special box built for a prized purchase, or get Pete's brace repaired below decks. Once I had a pair of white pants that needed to be bleached because of mud on a trail. I asked our steward for some bleach. He said nothing but soon the cabin captain appeared. Next, here came Willem. I explained my problem. His reply was, "Not on my carpet, you don't get bleach." He took the stained pants away with him and they came back from the laundry, good as new.

SOUTH KOREA—CHEJU CITY

MARCH 22ND My poor husband cannot go ashore today. He really is in pain. Lynn Anderson goes with me, using his ticket. She is a good sport and we enjoy the bright breezy day on Cheju Island. The bus is big and comfortable and we become adept at getting on and off. We walk at about the same speed. She makes the day fun with her quick wit.

Our thirty-two-year-old tour guide, Stephanie, has flown an hour from Seoul to Cheju City to escort us. The caves that are one of their most publicized features turn into an ordeal because of hundreds of Japanese tourists. Stephanie warns us that they will push us out of the way without speaking and so they do. As we go through the endless uninteresting caves, one little woman in red leans into my left side persistently. I lose patience and decide to push back just to see what will happen. I am much taller and just as stubborn as she is and she finally backs off. She is a special annoyance but there are hundreds more just like her, stopping short in the path right in front of us or pushing their way past. A few minutes later, here comes the little woman in red for another try. As the steady pressure on my side begins again, I resist once more. Suddenly she gives a loud hiss between her teeth—a neat condemnation of my actions. I let her win this time. She triumphantly marches ahead, a chicken who beat out a turkey.

Our next stop is a magnificent bonsai garden. There are two hundred or more miniature potted trees of many species sited along paths beneath tall trees among rocks. Ficus, azalea, oaks and pines, flowering quince and crab have each been nurtured for decades to an artistic shape. Many have not leafed out yet in the early spring weather, but all hold the promise of leaves and flowers as days grow longer. The open shade of the tall pine trees shelters them from hot sun. Strong winds do not penetrate here. The bonsais are beautiful even in their barren state. They hold the promise of life.

Our lunch of Korean food is bountiful and similar to the Chinese lunches we have been enjoying. This meal has lots of cold salads, some with curly tentacles of squid and other delicacies. I stick to fish, chicken, beef and foods I can identify. We do not eat cold dishes as a rule on shore but have plenty to eat with the hot foods. Both Lynn and I had looked forward to beer with lunch and she offers to buy, but we change our minds when we discover it is $8 per bottle.

After lunch and a short bus ride, we hop down steep steps to sea level to see a fishing village museum. There are perhaps a dozen small thatched houses with dirt floors that were lived in until thirty years ago. Now they demonstrate a former way of life. One of the tiny huts has a swift, a hackle, a small loom, cards and a spinning wheel, echoes of a weaver. Since I wove for twenty years, I am tuned in to the actions and spirit of other weavers. It is so right that she sat here, near the rolling sea, calmly throwing her shuttle and drawing the beater, waiting for the men to return. The soft long sweep of the ocean to the tumbled black rocks gives the village a peaceful atmosphere. Japanese tourists haven't heard about this place yet, for they are not obliterating every other impression with their pushy presence.

JAPAN—NAGASAKI

MARCH 23ʳᴰ What unthinking sadist would hire a Japanese drummer to pound his huge drum right outside the ship at 7:30 in the morning? We are docked on the street in Nagasaki with the drum shattering the peace of the day. It is amazing that one man can pound with such ferocity.

"Raining on earth means crying in heaven, my mother once told me," is a line by an unknown poet. It describes Nagasaki today. We board buses in the pouring rain of early spring—the kind of rain that makes the flowering trees bloom. The Glover Museum is our first stop, on top of a high hill in the center of the city. Our bus parks at the bottom of a long, winding street. Getting to the house means a slow walk past dozens of shops, up the hill in the rain. The wet walks are slippery. When we get to the top of the street, we find stairs and escalators and then more stairs to the top. Pete struggles gamely up, even in the lightly falling rain. He feels some better today and tries hard not to let his shoulder bother him.

The Glover mansion was built more than a hundred years ago. What a spectacular view it must have had before the harbor was developed. The charming Victorian house and Mr. Glover's Japanese wife are said to have been the inspiration for Puccini's opera, *Madame Butterfly*. An airy room with three walls of French doors open to the rain is beautifully furnished. The Glovers must have led a comfortable life here, high on this hill. We see a performance of kimono-clad geishas later in the day. The colors of their kimonos, their grace and complete femininity remind me of the opera and of the contemporary version, *Miss Saigon*.

Our most important visit of the day is to the museum commemorating the Nagasaki atom bomb. The epicenter of the bomb's destruction has been left empty with a tall black obelisk as a memorial. The nearby museum is a new, modern, efficient and well-presented horror. Photos of fried babies and burned elderly residents, tumbled buildings and twisted metal are sharp reminders of events Pete and I can recall. He doesn't come inside and I am happy for that. One aspect of the museum annoys many of the passengers. Nowhere in all the displays is the attack on Pearl Harbor even mentioned. In fact, one of the bus guides acknowledges that she never knew about the attack on our navy that December Sunday in 1941 until she was in her twenties. Our American Navy veterans are especially annoyed at the one-sided presentation. One friend sees me as he leaves the memorial. Because of his own feelings about WW II, he chants the familiar football cheer, "Hit 'em again, hit 'em again, harder, harder!" War is a tragedy for both sides. No-one wins.

By the time we return to the ship, Pete has broken out in a bright red rash on his left chest, under his left arm and on his back. He is in considerable pain, even after hydrocodone. We head right to the infirmary for a diagnosis of these new symptoms. Both Dr. Wass and Dr. Reimer agree: shingles. We are relieved, in a way. The pain and rash are apparently typical of this disease. The virus must have lain dormant in his system for years since he had chicken pox as a child. The doctor prescribes famver, which is supposed to help reduce the severity of the attack if it is administered in the first twenty-four hours after the rash becomes evident.

JAPAN—KAGOSHIMA

MARCH 24TH I fell in love today with the town of Chiran, thirty miles south of Kagoshima. Eight years ago when we were in Japan we saw Buddhist temple after temple. I was looking for the Japan of garden books, of the architecture that fired Frank Lloyd Wright, of Zen sensitivity, of beauty of form and proportion. Today we find it.

Chiran is a former fortified village where Samurai warriors built homes 250 years ago. An area warlord gave groups of them permission to build a ring of villages around his province to act as a perimeter defense. Chiran is one of those villages. It has had intense attention for all the years since then. Some houses have been preserved and a few of them are open to the public.

The street where the Samurai houses are located is as stark as a tunnel, with high stone walls and thick green podacarpus hedges rising above the grey stone. Entering through a roofed wooden gate, we follow stepping stones a few feet straight ahead, turn right and pass through a second gate. There is a small yard enclosing an unpainted wooden house with overhanging thatched roof. The eaves are thick with bound rice straw. They hang low, sheltering the building. The house has sliding screen walls, fitted tatami mats and an air of tranquillity. Gloom obscures the high ceilings.

A garden surrounds the house. A gravel sea is encircled by tufted pine trees, rocks and shrubs that will flower later in spring. In one corner dry rocks are carefully arranged to suggest a waterfall. A tall hedge runs all around the garden, trimmed in undulating waves to mimic the mountain range looming in the distance. The shapes of the contrasting plants must be wonderful in the snow. This atmosphere suggests the wood block prints Japanese artists are known for.

A second garden has a tall uneven hedge, with a sinuous coil of fat green shrubs in front. Our guide tells us the thick coil is azalea bushes which will flower pink next month. Here and there on the gravel in front of the azaleas are stone stands, a foot or so tall. The family places their collection of bonsai trees on these stands when they are in perfect condition to admire. Even though there are two dozen of us in the garden, an air of tranquillity prevails. Perhaps the sense of proportion is what makes me feel so calm.

Samurais were fearless warriors who fought with great bravery. Our guide says the warrior would sit in his house and contemplate his symbolic forest with mountains, flowers and waterfall while he wrote poetry. Some of their descendants still live here. I wish I could see one of these gardens alone with time to absorb the silence and the calm of the proportions.

As we hike back to the bus through the little village, we walk along a stone-sided trough that runs next to the sidewalk. Through it is channeled a little stream and in the stream Japanese gold fish are swimming. The street is lined with spare tufted pine trees, with black branches and flat pillows of pine needles. Everything about this village seems to have been planned by a sensitive hand.

The village of Chiran has a dark side as well. On the way out of town we pass a Zero airplane enshrined in a park. Next to it is a stone tablet commemorating the deaths of young men from a nearby air base who gave their lives in Kamikaze attacks on US ships. Not surprisingly, the descendants of the Samurai tradition carried their heroism into World War II in their suicide attacks on our navy. They left from this place of tranquillity on their errand of death.

Our second stop this day is at Ido garden—quite a different place. These gardens are extensive and frame the view of Kagoshima harbor and the nearby active volcano. Long lines of Rotterdam's passengers are seated on wooden benches watching a tea ceremony in progress. When my turn to sit comes, we are offered sweet pastel flowers made of sugar and gelatin to nibble. These sweets traditionally offset the slightly bitter taste of the green tea. Young women in colorful kimonos offer each of us a rough pottery bowl half full of foamy green sludge. I sip hesitantly. The flavor is not unpleasant but the texture reminds me of the slime in the bottom of my grandmother's lily pond. I can't drink much.

As we prepare to sail from the harbor, another drumming performance is given on the dock—a much better time of day for the show. An enormous drum on a cart, probably eight feet in diameter and twelve feet long is assaulted in unison by two strong male drummers. Six men play smaller versions and one plays a keyboard. The vibrations of the drumming cause sound to carom off nearby buildings. It is an exciting intensely personal rhythm that crescendos and calms in unison. The drummers are dressed in white and several of them wear wild red wigs. I'm not sure of the significance of this costume but we saw dolls in souvenir shops that were similarly dressed. Joann and Bill Blackburn join us on the balcony for the performance and to watch the ship sail away.

* * * * *

The Hat Lady is a more sympathetic figure these days; all her exuberance is gone. Her husband died one night and she is now traveling on alone. The fact that she has such poor vision makes her life difficult. Passengers take turns leading her when she seems confused. She is being invited to join nearby tables for dinner occasionally. She comes to dinner bare-headed more often than not. We are carrying his body back to Los Angeles where she says he will be cremated. She says she will return to the southwest by herself.

JAPAN—OSAKA

MARCH 25TH The last time we were in Japan, eight years ago, we departed very disappointed tourists—too many Buddhists, too many tempura lunches. One dinner of Kobe steak with Marcia and Morrie from California had been lots of fun but expensive. We try to make better choices this trip but there still is a shadow on the day. Pete isn't well enough to go ashore so Lynn Anderson and I leave the ship at 8 AM. The bus ride to Kyoto takes more than an hour on a Sunday morning. We never really leave the city atmosphere. The congestion stretches all the way from one city to the other.

Our goal is Nijo Castle, built in 1603. The central building is set inside walls that have huge tile-roofed gates and is surrounded by trees and gardens. We all have to remove our shoes and put them in bins with numbers while we walk through the building in our stocking feet. It is a cold day. I am glad I wore heavy hiking socks. The ceilings are high, gloomy with age, but still showing colorful paintings. Each dark cypress building is surrounded by a hall around the exterior, so we walk by all the rooms, but are not allowed inside. The rooms are floored with tatami mats. There are lovely shoji screens painted four hundred years ago with simple but elegant subjects. On four of the big panels in one huge room, a single pine tree spreads its green branches in a bonsai shape against a gold leaf background. The ceilings are intricate with gold leaf and colorful designs.

A surprise feature of this building are the "nightingale" floors. Underneath they are fitted to a moving peg that keeps them tight except when walked upon. The broad wooden boards sing or squeak when people walk over them. What an ingenious warning system! No-one would sneak up on the residents without warning.

In some spaces figures dressed in ceremonial garments give an idea of how the rooms might have looked during court functions. One tale describes why the men's pants had such long trousers—they would trail behind a man's feet by a yard. In order to walk, the courtier would have to hold his pants up with each hand and then he would have no hands free to reach for a sword so he could harm the noble. The story is also told that the noble reviewed girls presented for his approval. If he selected one, he took the cup of tea from her hands to signal his choice.

The surrounding garden is lovely with huge trees propped with poles or surrounded by a network of poles to hold them upright. Everything is clean and pruned and lovingly cared for. To keep the old trees shaped and groomed to an exact size, we are told the gardeners remove new needles by hand. Can this be the same country that the pushy woman in red came from?

* * * * *

We don't leave Osaka until noon the second day, so in the morning we go to the mall in the Terminal. Pete hasn't been out much lately and he is glad to get off the ship. Next to the pier there is a giant 350 foot Ferris wheel that overlooks the whole city. He gets on for a ride and spends a pleasant fifteen minutes. He reports that looking down on the Rotterdam from that height makes it appear small. After his ride he has a big smile on his face.

Houston Witherspoon was taken to the Osaka hospital today with pneumonia. John from Cruise Specialists spends a lot of time helping him understand what is happening. Houston will try to rejoin the trip in Honolulu in ten days.

JAPAN—TOKYO

MARCH 28TH We faxed Yash and Kyoko Sano, Rotary friends from thirty-two years ago that we would be in Tokyo today. Eight years ago when we visited Tokyo, Yash was in year-long mourning for the death of his mother and could not see us. But today he and Kyoko are at the gangplank about nine-thirty. We show them every bit of the ship. Yash takes lots of photos. By eleven we are ready to leave and a little confused about where we will go and what we will see. Yash's English is somewhat obscured by his Japanese pronunciation and Kyoko is shy about her's. But we bumble on, hoping we are agreeing to the right things and not quite sure.

We take a long and expensive cab ride to the Asakusa View Hotel where we go up to the twenty-seventh floor. If it were a clear day, we could see Mt. Fuji from here, but not today. The sky is overcast and rain is threatening. Yash asks whether we would prefer Chinese or French food. I feel a brief moment of disappointment that we will not eat Japanese.

We agree on lunch in the French restaurant, the unexpected ultimate eating experience of the whole World Cruise. The food on the ship is consistently excellent but this is delicious and exquisite—French with Japanese attention to the artistic arrangement of color and design. The first course is tempura fried white bait—tiny two-inch-long whole little minnows dipped in perfectly seasoned delicate batter, served hot and crisp in a little mound. No sauce is served; none is needed. I would have preferred to eat them with chopsticks. A fork seems too coarse for such delicacy, but there isn't a chopstick to be seen in the restaurant.

The next course is sashimi tuna—raw fish slices presented plain with one leaf of beet green, one stalk of steamed green onion and a wee mound of dressed endive. Following comes a vibrant blue soup plate with bright yellow fragrant broth in which are floating small transparent fish eggs. I know Pete doesn't understand what he is eating and he laps it up.

The men have steak for their entree while Kyoko and I order steamed dorado (fish). It comes as two small strips of perfectly cooked white flesh, covered with a paper thin slice of some vegetable, a transparent pancake, two snow peas, one half a tiny two-inch-long root vegetable, poached, two stalks of green spinach and a golden yellow sauce scattered with delicate bits of chopped red bell pepper. Every bite proves that food can taste as good as it looks. Sublime is the best word to describe both presentation and taste.

We don't need any more food, but dessert comes. It is another visual and sensual delight. There is a small oval of chocolate mousse—rich and nearly bitter, another oval scoop of vanilla bean ice cream, four perfect blueberries, two jumbo red raspberries, a length-wise half slice of kiwi fruit, a flower shape of bright orange sugar-glazed nectarine and a two-inch square of apricot and pastry cream tart. As full as we are, we eat every bite with slow pleasure. This is one of the most memorable meals of our lifetimes.

After lunch we walk in the spring rain through a flower arched street past hundreds of small shops. The effect of the flowers takes away our concern at getting wet. At the far end is the Asakusa Kannon temple. Apparently the pleasure-loving atmosphere has prevailed in this neighborhood for hundreds of years. We walk and walk, passing Diane and Marshall Rife from the ship and a Japanese friend of theirs.

During the walk in the rain, Pete drops his afternoon pill for shingles. He knew it was a $13 pill, so down on his hands and knees he went in the dirt of the alley. Before I could stop him, he popped the pill into his mouth. If he comes down with something worse, I won't be a bit surprised. Yash and Kyoko realize this part of the day is hard for us and soon we are in a taxi, having another $50 ride back to the ship.

Yash leaves us an autographed copy of his new book on folding origami dog breeds. He also gives us a copy of the monthly origami magazine he publishes and a beautiful blue cotton tablecloth. Our gift to them of World Cruise 2000 coffee cups seems inadequate and useless.

Peggy and Gene Masica had the pleasure of a visit from their grandson, Mike, today. He is stationed on the aircraft carrier, Kitty Hawk, nearby and is an F18 pilot, due to be deployed to the Straits of Taiwan very soon. It was lucky for them that he was still here. We ran into them on the ship this morning. He looks much too young to have graduated from Annapolis and to be flying a multi-million dollar aircraft. The smiles on their faces said how happy they all were to be together.

One of the treats of this cruise has been getting to know two regular navy men, Chuck Anderson and Gene Masica. We've eaten dinner with them and their wives and Moe and Sylvia for nearly three months now. These guys share a love for and the language of the sea. Polio struck Chuck when he was young, ending his naval career, but his heart is still there. Gene Masica went to the Naval Academy and became a submarine captain. He and Chuck speculate every morning about the condition of the ship and have some informed ideas about how she is sailing. Conversations at dinner frequently turn to naval matters and to ships and the sea. We learn a lot from listening to the humor and experiences of these two. Gene has a pugnacious jaw and a twinkle in his eye. His wife, Peggy, is a patient lifelong navy wife. Lynn Anderson is a cheerful and consistently positive person. We really have enjoyed our dinner table. Tim and Charlotte Nault were with us for a month, as were Jackie and Beth for the first month. They were all a good fit too.

We sail from Tokyo at nine at night and shortly afterward the ocean gets rough. We had had rain in Tokyo and Yash and Kyoko had said a big storm was predicted. Wind begins to blow and the ship bumps all night. We have been blessed with so much calm sailing. Now we remember we really are on a ship. The first hour in bed I try to find a way to sleep where my body doesn't roll around. Then, as the storm worsens and the movement becomes more unpredictable, I begin to clutch Pete for comfort and an anchor. Chewing a couple of the meclazine tablets that the Front Office gives out calms my tummy tremors. I give up trying to get comfort from Pete and drift off to sleep.

* * * * *

The motion lasts through the next day. A scheduled cocktail party in the Crow's Nest is canceled and we make it to dinner with great difficulty. The rocking and pitching continues the second night. About one-thirty in the morning there is a horrendous crash that wakes us both up. Pete sits right up in bed, loudly proclaiming, "I don't like this. I want to get off this ship tomorrow." That makes me smile because we are at sea tomorrow. He calms down some and we go back to sleep, but the next morning, March 30th, we learn that a huge wave has dented the bow of the Rotterdam. It will be Midway Island before anyone can get a look at the damage from the outside.

MIDWAY ISLAND

SATURDAY, APRIL 1ST We arrive at Midway Island later today, site of the famous World War II battle. As we sail along on a windy blue sea, we must be right in the area of the famous sea battle. Admiral Yamamoto's fleet was engaged at sea before it could invade the tiny islands. Visiting the actual site makes the era and battle more fresh in our minds.

Midway is a National Park now where the US Park Service is in charge. Our lecturer, a young woman, outlines the history of the island, especially as the turning point of the war in the Pacific. She shows the film, *Midway*. Her talk carries us up to the present with slides of the bird, sea turtle and monk seal population. Huge numbers of albatross, boobies and terns live on the beaches. Turtles and seals reproduce here. Although the Navy just left three years ago, many of the buildings have already been pulled down so Midway can be returned to a natural condition.

It is undecided whether we will get ashore. There is a narrow cut into the inner lagoon through the coral atoll and Rotterdam sails like a box kite in the wind. The weather of the past four days has been so rough that we have spent more effort traveling up hills and through troughs than making forward progress. We are due in for a brief four hours—from two to six PM, and we must leave before poor light makes it impossible to exit the lagoon. Shore tickets for two hour visits are passed out because the number of people on the island at any one time is carefully restricted.

Rumors have been flying about what caused the damage to the ship the other night—we hit a whale—we will all be flown home from Hawaii. The ship will go into drydock on the west coast. We hit a loose container from a big container ship. A thousand minds are speculating. Cruise Specialist's chat time every sea day is a great time to calm fears and put the most implausible rumors to rest.

Pete had a really bad night last night. He was sitting up in a chair at three AM, in pain and annoyed with himself. I fixed him a cold wet towel to put under his left arm, got him one of my pain pills and stayed awake until he finally went to sleep. He saw both physicians yesterday afternoon. They say he is responding normally, the famver is doing its job and he should be over the worst of the illness by the time we reach home. These past ten days have changed the trip for him and yet it may be better to be sick here than at home. He's under no requirement to keep a normal schedule now and can do what he wishes. One of the best assets is that the telephone rarely rings.

Midway Island turns out to be the ultimate April Fool's Day trick. Like Tristan da Cunha, we pause within sight of the ring of coral, the turquoise waters and the low tree-covered island. Finally the Captain says the wind speed is above fifteen knots, too stiff for us to enter the channel. We loiter at sea, transferring two ill passengers to an old navy diesel tug that comes out to meet us. Both passengers are on stretchers. They will be medi-vacced out by the Coast Guard right to Honolulu. A few boxes of souvenirs are transferred to Rotterdam for fear some of us might miss our chance to shop. We sail on, flat-topping the ocean waves with recurring thuds.

This ship reminds me of the old flat bottom boat we used to have at Smoke Lake. We called her "Matilda." She hauled a lot of lumber and an iron stove five miles up the lake but they had to run her ashore in rough weather or she would have gone under. A new hull design gives Rotterdam the same ability to haul a big load but in rough water, she rides like a scow. We wish passenger capacity would make way for a comfortable ride, especially for World Cruises.

One event brightens our outlook. We are invited to a special Friendship Dinner in the Odyssey Dining Room. Anne and Norm Cottman, Lou Lamoreaux and Jean Aylesworth entertain enough guests to fill the whole alternate dining room. The room brings so much to the pleasure of the evening—it is all gilt, glass, and windows, with expert waiters and an intimate atmosphere. Table settings are lovely and glassware is delicate. The dinner consists of shrimp and caviar as an appetizer, carrot and pumpkin soup, a green salad and lobster folded into a chicken breast as an entree. With wines, good talk, and a delicious dessert, we have a bell-ringer of an evening. The hospitality of friends lightens our mood.

UNITED STATES—HONOLULU, HAWAII

APRIL 4TH As we calmly and majestically sail through the harbor entrance to Honolulu, a fireboat follows us to our berth. Three towering arches of water drape curtains of mist over the beautiful blue green waters. A helicopter chop-chops overhead and someone tosses bright flower petals so that they float down all around the ship. A musical group plays "Sweet Leilani" as the thrusters push us to our berth. After the very rough seas, concern about the damage to the ship and the long period since Tokyo, we are all relaxed and reassured by our arrival safe in harbor. We dock on the starboard side so the damage will be visible.

The band is a group of volunteers who leave their jobs to greet every ship that arrives in Honolulu. Singers are dressed in red and yellow and their songs echo around the ship. A hula dancer weaves her graceful dance. There are a thousand golden leis to be given to the passengers. Even the longshoremen are dressed in blue, yellow and red shirts. Land looks good to our sea-weary eyes. It is our first view of the United States in almost fifteen weeks.

We go by shuttle bus to the Ala Moana mall to shop for American products. Being able to find familiar necessities of life, like toothpaste and bottled water and ball point pens is a treat. We have a fast food lunch and even that tastes wonderful. Taxiing back to the ship increases the cost of what we bought, but there is satisfaction in paying normal prices.

We see the damage to the bow of the ship today. We already

had been down to the forward part of Dolphin Deck where we saw the dent in the I-beam. Now that we can see the outside of the bow, the dent is obvious, but not deep. None of the plating is fractured. Everyone says we will get a Coast Guard inspection before we can proceed. The best guess is that a rogue wave damaged our bow that night.

The cocktail hostesses are entertaining again. We receive an invitation for a party on a casual dress night, "Dress code—Formal attire." Pete is uncomfortable for when we arrive in the dining room in our formal regalia, the whole dining room is on notice that we were invited to a special event and they were not. By this time in the trip, many of us are getting a little weary of dressing formally. We have had twenty-six formal dress evenings already.

Houston Witherspoon has recently returned to the ship. He was sent ashore at Osaka when his health was declining. He flew to Honolulu, where he recuperated enough to join the ship again yesterday. He will celebrate his 100th birthday on the eighth of December this year. He has had nearly forty World Cruises and is a dependable sight on these trips. There is an early celebration among his shipboard friends. The celebration overwhelms him and he regresses to a wheelchair again, but he is back on his feet the following day. He is a dear bandy legged man who wears a big brimmed hat square on top of his head. Pete has had several talks with him about his philanthropy to a college in Asheville, where he underwrote a new science building.

The ship may have sailed all the way from Tokyo on one propeller according to our navy friends. We eat breakfast at the windows against the stern quite often and the condition of the ship and sea traffic is most of the conversation. The two "old salts" keep up with shipboard conditions. Gene Masica is upstairs by six most mornings and has his group of buddies who talk things over. Moe is part of that group some of the time. He and Sylvia go to bed by ten at night and start their day sometimes as early as three AM. Peggy and Lynn attend crafts class held sea days, where they have made tote bags, evening bags and done needlepoint. Pete, when he feels well, goes to all the men's sporting events and they are a source of stories. My group of people to talk with share a few minutes conversation in passing.

As a rule we prefer to eat meals in the dining room where moderate amounts of food are brought to the table for us. It's easier than trying to manage a tray. The conversations are more important than the quantity of food, even though we still can order as much as we wish.

Most of the passengers get off in Los Angeles in a week. Packing to go home is a curse. The same number of clothes has to go home as came on board and the same number of suitcases is available. The fruits of shopping trips and $400 worth of "ship's amenities" are some of the unknowns. On a World Cruise, more than on shorter cruises, we are presented with a variety of logo items by the cruise line. This year's list includes Bushnell binoculars, letter writing folders, a beautiful book on Antarctica, two ethnic cuisine cookbooks, coffee mugs, a jigsaw puzzle, Kenyan stone masks, duffel bags and a transparent world globe the size of a large golf ball. The ship lists the value of these items. We have to itemize them on our US Customs forms and include their value in our exemption. If we keep everything we are given, and we have two sets of all of it, it takes up our full US exemption for being out of the country.

We all shop for treasures as we travel. There is a list of developing countries where items grown, manufactured and sold are duty free. Luckily that list includes most of the places where I bought gifts. We hope we get a kind custom's agent. We will have been out of the country nearly four months and $400 seems a small allowance for each person.

* * * * *

One of most meaningful experiences of this cruise has been a writing class with Carol Dovi. There have been from six to twenty of us on hand in spite of awkward scheduling of the classes. Our meeting time is the same hour that the major speaker of the day is giving a lecture in the Queen's Lounge. We have had to forego talent like Malachy McCourt, author and raconteur, to sit in Carol's room and talk about writing. She gives us several blocks of time to write small subjects and we get a chance to hear a little that the other participants can do. Several of the women are published authors, including Adeline Garner Shell. Carol carefully encourages each one of us at our own level and gives us the names of books she has found helpful. She gives pointers for the process of finding an agent and a publisher.

The highlight of the class is the day Malachy McCourt comes to regale us for an hour with his stories—a special effort he makes just for twenty of us. He is a large man with a vast expanse of stomach that sticks out when he lays back in his chair. His wee blue eyes sparkle as he tells of his drinking and longshoremen days. He describes the process he followed to get his recent book, *A Monk Swimming*, published and the daily habits he is governed by as he gets his writing done. He says that "writing is a muscle. Exercise it!"

McCourt's blue eyes snap as he speaks of honesty in writing. He explains with pain one of the most formative events in his childhood. Their father abandoned him, his three brothers, and their mother when he was ten. The family had nothing and nowhere to turn. A cousin, a beast of a man who beat the children and sexually abused their mother, gave them a home. The children could hear the noises as they lay awake in their own bed at night. McCourt says it would have been easier not to tell what he knew about that time in their lives, but it would not have been honest to omit it. Because those events had such an impact on the formation of his own character, he tells the story as it happened, with the wide-eyed horror of a listening child in his eyes.

A little lady who lives near us on Verandah deck has been nicknamed "Twilight" by Perry, the piano player. She is plump and black-haired, short and walks as if she used to walk more freely. Her Verandah cabin for one person costs 160% of the regular full fare or nearly $70,000 for one person. She says her son worries that she is spending too much traveling on World Cruises—this is her third—but she is having a wonderful time. She looks up defiantly and says "What better way is there to spend it?" I see her in the Lido today with two hamburgers and salad for lunch and she relishes every bite.

Our stop in Honolulu turns into a serendipitous event. Since the ship is late coming in, the Captain decides to cancel Maui the next day and stay a day and a half in Honolulu. The winds and rough seas have made us all glad to have a night in port and a calm quiet bed. The weather may seem bad to the Hawaiians—some of them wear jackets and sweaters—but it is balmy and warm to us.

UNITED STATES— KAILUA-KONA

APRIL 6TH This is the last official port for the World Cruise which officially ends in Los Angeles on April 11. Everyone is packing and shipping excess baggage home. Pete and I have decided to stay on board another two weeks, all the way to Ft. Lauderdale. A special low fare has been offered, if we move to another cabin. Those extra weeks mean a complete circumnavigation of the world for us and will give Pete a little more time to recover from his illness. We are missing nearly two weeks of our children's visit in Florida, but they will be there for three days after we get back.

There has not been a time yet in this one hundred and three days on board when I have been restless or wishing to be at home. It is so easy to let someone else make the bed, cook, and clean for us. We meet many interesting people. We feel so fortunate to be able to be here that we won't let any unpleasant event interfere with our good time.

It is a little overcast and the sea is bumpy again as we take a small boat along the Kona coast. I am always reluctant to sign up for more water travel when we do so much anyway. But this little trip is fun. There is a blonde young woman with buck teeth who dances the hula and plays the ukulele. Her teeth become secondary with the grace of her performance. Cups of pineapple juice are free and popular. Lots of free snacks are available to keep sea sickness away. I enjoy my first bag of Fritos in three months. We sail down the coast a while and then back up for three hours. Pete goes back to the ship and I go to Hilo Hattie's and buy a green muumuu. I load up on Kona coffee and macadamias.

We enter an elevator on the way to lunch on the ship in Kona to find a surprise. The couple on the elevator are all dressed up. He is wearing a tux at one-thirty in the afternoon. She looks lovely in an ankle length beige dress with beautiful lace embroidery in a deep inset around the hem. We say something that causes them to respond that they just got married. Pete does just the right thing and asks if he may kiss the bride. She offers her cheek to him and I shake hands with both of them as they get off, on the way to find a bar open at this time of day where they can have a celebratory toast.

Lester and Helen Rosenblatt invite us for cocktails tonight. He is a bright guy, nearly eighty years old, independent of spirit, with attentive eyes and one of the foremost Naval Architects in the United States. Helen is a pretty little lady with a sweet Virginia accent. He makes her birthday special by giving her a lovely diamond bracelet. He loves to swap jokes with Pete: the worse they are, the better he likes them.

Moe and Sylvia give a cocktail party with Stewart and Cele. We had suggested we all give one early in the cruise, but they refused, saying they didn't know anyone. Now that we have been on board together for so long, they feel better about the idea. They have a nice party in the Ambassador. Cele wears a necklace made of gold stars. I ask if it is meant to symbolize the Dallas Stars, the hockey team. Apparently, it is not.

Our tablemates are delightful, even after this many dinners together. Moe and Sylvia opt out occasionally but far less often than we thought they would. Andersons and Masicas share running jokes about the Anderson's $7 Vietnamese elephant that will cost them $70 more in packing and shipping to get home. Gene Masica demands that I include a pornographic chapter in this memoir. Since he was a sailor, I suggest that he write the chapter for me from his firsthand experiences.

Our jewel of a table steward in the dining room is the tall handsome Indonesian named Suke. We have enjoyed his care for nearly a hundred days. He is quick-witted. Part way through the trip he said he had a book of American idioms. That gave us a challenge and each day we tried to give him a new one. Lester Rosenblatt offers one of the worst. It takes three embarrassing explanations before we can get Suke to understand both the meaning and that he really should never say it to anyone he respects.

We miss one of the highlights of the trip tonight. It was advertised that we would sail past Haleakala at midnight so we could see the red hot lava hitting the sea. It is said to be a spectacular show. But the Captain decided we didn't have enough time to make that pass.

Most passengers only have four more days on board. Returning by ship to Ft. Lauderdale solves our problem with excess baggage. Otherwise we would have had to ship more than half of our accumulation home, at 30 cents a pound. The ship has made it difficult for the women who bring more outfits than a clothing store has. They all have racks tied to hooks in their cabins to extend their closet space and they seldom wear the same thing twice. In the past, Rotterdam has carried extra baggage back to Ft. Lauderdale. When we visit the engine room, we see that there is plenty of space available for luggage, but perhaps liability is the problem. This year, after the trip had begun, the ship announced they could not do that any longer. Tempers flared as passengers thought about the ramifications.

We say goodbye to Larry, the single man who sat at a nearby table. He preferred his solitude. Sometimes we shook him out of his isolation by buying him a cocktail or sending him a glass of wine. He managed to make the whole World Cruise after having been sent home for medical reasons on two other tries. He bought a small gold globe during this last week when he was sure he would complete the trip and has been wearing it on a gold chain with a sparkle in his eyes.

We were telling a friend about how much it would cost us to stay on board two more weeks. As he said, "Stay on board. You can eat that much every day!"

Debbie Reynolds is the entertainer tonight. She is as old as we are and yet she looks great, is in good voice and is very funny. Her performance is a triumph. When she was coming to the ship, somehow a car door caught her in the left cheek and she wears a Band-Aid on her face. However, her exuberance goes on for an hour and fifteen minutes. We all remember our teen-age years when she was a heartthrob.

There have been other wonderful name entertainers over the hundred days. Schecky Greene was funny; John Davidson looked great and sang as well as he did in the old days. Pat Boone was a pleasant relic from the days of white buck shoes. Other entertainers were unknown to us, but gave great shows. Especially funny was the man who blew up a balloon to enormous size and then proceeded to get into it so that nothing was showing except his feet. As he moved around the stage, the absurdity of it all struck us.

UNITED STATES— LOS ANGELES

APRIL 11TH The official end of the World Cruise has arrived. Los Angeles is foggy and very American looking. Everything is orderly and clean. We said goodbye to Andersons and Masicas last night and Craddocks called this morning but we weren't up yet. I haven't felt well for a day or two, getting Sylvia's cold, I think. The move to the next cabin is overwhelming as we need to box up books and gifts, sort slips for customs, separate clothes for cold weather and pack those, while we keep warm weather duds available, including formal wear for three nights. Fellow passengers give us wine that they can't carry home and we already have a boxful left over. Overall, there are twelve suitcases and six boxes, more than the Lower Prom cabin we are to move into can handle. We get lucky and are able to store the excess in an empty cabin for the next two weeks. That big bottle of Amaretto is still with us, unopened. If we can get it through customs, we will be happy to have it at home.

All of a sudden, the atmosphere changes. Nine hundred passengers get off; all the familiar faces leave. The World Cruise is over. Our good friends are gone. Just forty-five from the World remain, heading to Florida and New York. About six hundred new people come on board for the two-week trip. We all feel disoriented. There are new officers, a new Voice from the Bridge, Captain Pieter Bos this time, and a new Cruise Director, Edwin Rojas, is announcing the program each day. New staff makes us even more aware of how much things have changed.

Another big adjustment is our new dinner table, the big round table in the center of the main floor, where Frank Clyne, Diana Weiss and the Bayshores have been for the whole trip. Nancy Walsh has been with them for a few weeks. Besides us, Gene and Rosemarie Zitani, who have just come on board, have joined the table. Chief Engineer Bert Boone is there formal nights.

The atmosphere is different. Julia in the Internet Cafe is stressed with the challenges and misunderstandings of the new passengers. When she was called on stage at the farewell for the World, she got enough cheers from the crowd to make her feel good. Julia is thrilled with the whole trip. She bought hand-carved chairs, tables, and lamps from Thailand and as she says, "every boat of every size and description" that she saw. She has worked hard to make things work for all the varied stages of passenger familiarity with the Internet. Charges for the Internet have dropped a third now that the World is over. We are so grateful to have had e-mail during the long voyage.

Two weeks ago we called cabin 3319 to make sure everything worked before we accepted it as our new cabin. The previous inhabitants said it was fine, no problem. Everything worked well when we moved in Tuesday, but since yesterday there has been no air circulating from the overhead vent at all. How can we get so lucky? Last night we were blown on all night by a big box fan on top of the TV set, like we had part of the time during the main part of the cruise. But Albert, an accommodating Engineer, showed up promptly and fixed the problem in no time. So much equipment needs to work perfectly on a ship that it is no wonder something falls short occasionally.

MEXICO—CABO SAN LUCAS

APRIL 13TH We are lying at anchor off the endless sand beaches and hills of Baja California. As we sail past the cliffs through the Marlin Channel, we see how much Cabo San Lucas has grown in the three years since we have been here.

This sunny day is a contrast to our last visit. It was a promised port on the last voyage of Rotterdam V, but in 1997, we could do no more than tender a few VIP's ashore and continue on our way. A bad storm was threatening the western Mexican coast. In fact, that storm finally deluged Acapulco and other cities with torrential rain. We stayed far out to sea under endless grey skies and let the storm wreak its havoc. When we finally reached the Canal, things had quieted considerably and we were all restless after being ship-bound for ten days. World cruisers become accustomed to a missed port now and then due to tide or storm or politics, but short termers don't have much flex-time in their brief stay on board.

We have been to the glass factory and the hotels, so today we get off the ship and go to the souvenir shops on the dock. We are looking for a birthday gift for our three-year-old grandson. He is not interested in woven serapes, maracas, or garish pottery plates. When we return to the ship, we savor the atmosphere on board. Each day becomes a thing to be treasured as the cruise comes to slowly to an end.

MEXICO—ACAPULCO

APRIL 15TH A sweet curve of sea and shore lines the harbor. Warm breezes ruffle the palm trees. Turquoise water shines in the bay. Steep mountains ring the city and somewhere nearby are the beaches for which this city is famous. We have been here at least three times before and don't have any strong desire to see the sights again. We head for the B and B Silver Factory and shops to see about a few small last-minute gifts.

The taxi takes us on a tiny ride, through gates into a compound and to a building that looks like a bus station. A man opens the door for us and escorts us inside. He introduces himself as Benjamin and we tell him we only need small gifts. He suggests tanzanite. We refuse—just small gifts, we repeat. One thing leads to another. We buy a cross and chain for Wilma, pillboxes for the Dinner Bridge ladies, a key-shaped key ring for Martha, bracelets and money clips for the people at the office, a necklace and bracelet for Pete's sister, a letter opener for her husband, bracelets for the girls, a hair ornament for Kathy and a bracelet, necklace and calling card case for me. Then in a last mad impulse, we buy a sterling silver four-piece tea set for Wendy. We look at each other in disbelief. The stock market went way, way down yesterday and here we are spending money as if we had it. Pete reminds me that Microsoft has lost 25% of its value in the last week, between the lawsuit judgment and the kick the stock took yesterday. Everything else went down yesterday too. We will begin to be careful tomorrow. The sterling is duty-free because of the NAFTA trade agreement.

MEXICO— SANTA CRUZ-HUATULCO

APRIL 16TH Palm Sunday This is a development waiting to happen. The bus guide says the Mexican tourism agency began work here fifteen years ago. Beautiful roads snake across the mountains from beach to beach. We visit six lookout points, giving us long views over lonely beaches and surf. The earth is parched and dusty, trees are brown. Everything is bone dry. We drive past half a dozen hotel developments that are irrigated and landscaped but everything else looks like it is dying. It is hot. The rainy season begins in May and lasts through September. That is also the time of high heat and humidity when mildew multiplies. The rest of the year is dry. This place has not had a ship since January and yet they depend on tourism for their income. The Mexican development agency pays the locals to get them to move off the beaches and into town. It gives them a new house for making the move. The beaches are lovely little pockets of sand between rocky inlets. Many of the Indians took a lot of convincing to get them to leave their idyllic locations. The beaches look better to us too.

After a two hour bus ride—fortunately it is air-conditioned—we are given an hour to walk around the center of Las Crucecita. Shops lining the central square have garish T shirts, tote bags and hammocks for sale. There are families in the restaurants having lunch. Little children are seated in front of tall frozen-Margarita-size footed bowls of chocolate milk with a tall straw in each one. Each child has a look of total pleasure.

We sit on a bench in the shade of the central square. A young boy approaches, hoping to sell us hand-painted bookmarks. At two for three dollars, we buy fourteen. He is patient as we use our high school Spanish to add up the money. An older girl comes along to be sure we pay him the right amount. I give him $2 for himself and later, when I look back at him, he is waving the $2 in the air and kissing it as he cavorts with excitement. It takes little to make a child happy.

* * * * *

The ship is a different place since we left Los Angeles. The new crowd is younger and much noisier. Our dinner hour is cursed with a table of shrieking women nearby. We are glad they are having fun but it is unnerving to hear their boisterous and raucous behavior. Our table, all World Cruisers, wish they would have better manners. The cruise line must love this crowd. There is a lot more activity in the Casino and a crowd stays up late dancing and drinking. Bingo at $20 a card is played twice a day. Lots of action for the photographers makes them smile.

We are being served at one seating for dinner and there is only one performance of the show at 9:15. The evening meal is very slow because of all the congestion in the kitchen. Last night Pete and I ate at the Lido for dinner for the first time on the whole cruise. We had the same food as is served in the dining room, but with less noise, more scenery and quicker service. If you are not feeling well, that is the perfect solution.

COSTA RICA— PUERTO CALDERA

APRIL 18TH What does it take to have a perfect shore excursion? In a hot location, a comfortable bus with good air conditioning is one requirement. An attractive tour guide who knows her stuff makes the day interesting. A bus driver who uses care and good judgment is important. We have all these basics today as we tour Costa Rica from the tender dock at Puerto Caldera. This is our last scheduled shore excursion. This amazing trip is ending; Ft. Lauderdale is a week from today. Our drive into the mountains to Central Valley takes nearly three hours. Having no bathroom stops could have caused chaos with the earlier group of elderly passengers, but we seem to manage today.

At the Britt Coffee plantation, three actors guide us through the coffee growing and processing story with wit and humor. They explain that the beans are hand picked when they are red, aged in the sun, soaked and roasted. Outer husks are used as organic fertilizer. Roasting is done to three shades—light for gentle flavor, dark for robust flavor and dark almost to the point of burning for espresso. Coffee bushes grow in light shade under a canopy of legume-fixing trees that make the soil more fertile. Sunlight filters down; palm fronds sway in the slight breeze. The setting is pleasant.

For $4 we buy 12 oz. bags of the most aromatic and flavorful coffee I have ever tasted. Modern technology means we can order more from home on their web site. It can be ordered at $8 a bag plus shipping from www.cafebritt.com or 1.800.462.7488.

Our second stop is at the Swiss Travel Services' own facility for lunch. Salad, bar-b-que, fruit, bread and beer satisfy our hunger. The atmosphere is minimal although there is a band playing under the trees. We enjoy eating at a picnic table in the shade with Larry and Helen Kasman, World Cruisers we have not met previously.

At the end of the long ride back to the port, Anna, the tour guide, makes my day. She has given us lots of information about Costa Rica: why they have no army and how proud they are of their former president Arias, who won the Nobel Prize for peace. She brags about the high literacy rate and the happiness of the people. She talks about the main export of the country, coffee, and how much she enjoys a good cup.

But at the end of her story she surprises us all. She announces, "I am a God-believer." She tells us she hopes we come back to Costa Rica someday. But if we do not, she says she will see us in heaven. She announces with great conviction she will be at a table with her friends and we will each be welcome to come and join them. She will buy us each a cup of good coffee when we get there.

PANAMA CANAL—AGAIN

APRIL 20TH After Costa Rica, the Panama Canal comes again. This is the first time we have ever crossed it from west to east. Pete sees some new angles, especially toward the Carribbean side, where it is possible to stand in the bow and see three levels of the canal locks at once. It is a cool, lovely day, especially for Panama, where it has always been very hot and humid other times. The ship passes out Panama rolls in the dining room and on deck—a very sticky sweet roll with peach filling. It is difficult to judge what the condition of the canal is, now that Panama has been running it for four months. This is the first time we have ever had to anchor during our transit. We are held in Gatun Lake for a couple of hours. Captain Bos's voice on the speaker system seems impatient at the delay. But the crossing is completed without any other problem.

CURACAO—WILLEMSTAD

APRIL 22ND This is our very last port and we are still trying to find a birthday present for the three-year-old. The best we can do is a pair of wooden shoes, painted to look like ducks. We sit in the plaza alongside the ferry docks and wait for the pontoon bridge to close so we can cross back to the ship. As the minutes pass, we decide we had better order something or the owners will chase us out. At eleven o'clock in the morning, we order huge ice cream sundaes. We take the Ferry instead of waiting longer for the bridge.

Final packing takes two days, even though we have the majority of the bags and boxes packed and already in the cabin next door. In the end, we have twenty cases and boxes to cope with. When Pete goes up to the Customs Official with his slips in hand, the man gives him a smile and a wave. We get it all through, even the extra bottles.

This has been a memorable cruise. It is amazing and satisfying to know that we have been all the way around the world. Cruising is a splendid way to travel. We are many pounds more than when we came on board but we have enjoyed every minute of the trip. New friends from our cruise will be hooks to hang on to after the trip is over.

UNITED STATES—FT. LAUDERDALE

APRIL 26TH Our son, Dan and his friend, Rick Johnson arrive in time for breakfast in the Lido. After a tour of the ship, we get off about eleven. We are so late in leaving that we have a new experience. Our bags were left forlornly waiting on the floor of the warehouse, along with Kissing Annie's. She is always the last to get off and the line expects her to be late. But our bags have been sent to the impound area of Holland America. With a little confusion we assemble everything, with the exception of one duffel bag. It is identical to a bag every other World Cruise passenger owns and some little old lady has taken the wrong one. We swap with her on the way out of Ft. Lauderdale.

The last two weeks have been an afterglow of the World Cruise. They were pleasant but uneventful. We know now that the special atmosphere of a World Cruise disappears when a majority of the passengers goes home. Some of the officers and crew remain the same, but the mood was gone. The best part of the trip is the people we shared it with and this beautiful ship.

We have circumnavigated the world, all in the same direction, in one trip, by the same means of transportation. During a previous cruise, a representative of the Circumnavigation Society in New York defined what it took to be a member. Now we qualify. The one hundred and seventeen day voyage has left us both willing to go on forever and willing to get off. We are calm and happy and feel satisfied with what we have seen.

There are lessons to be assimilated when we have time to reflect. I remember the hopelessness of overpopulated India, the diligence and fierce pride of the Chinese, the poverty of Nosy Be´, Madagascar. In these already over-populated countries, such high rates of human reproduction foretell disasters like starvation and animal extinction far into the future. The problems of Africa and India are our problems, I know.

When we think of the happy times, we will remember the idyllic qualities of the Seychelles and Phuket, the perfection of Chiran, the intensity of Zanzibar. I am reinforced in my former opinion that Zanzibar is one of my most favorite places.

Four memorable meetings with young boys remain—the ten-year-old in Ecuador saying thank you for my $4 purchase; the Chinese boy in Tianjin dressed in yellow, speaking careful perfect English; the little three-year-old putting the peanut shells in the tub; and the young boy in the park in Las Crucecita, Mexico, who sold us carved bookmarks and then kissed the two dollars extra we gave him. We sign up for these cruises, never sure of what will happen or what we will see. We come home full of happy memories and with new friends.

The world is smaller than we think. We must not assume because our lives are good that everyone else is happy too. One of the reasons we love cruising is that we develop perspective about our world. We experience the vast spaces of ocean. We see the poverty of Third World countries and know their national policy is affected by that poverty. Health concerns in other parts of the world are our health concerns, now that there is so much air travel. Our understanding of differing life styles and religions is expanded. We wish we could get CNN World News at home as we do on the ship. Perhaps if we did, we Americans wouldn't be so provincial.

The trip has been long enough so that Pete is feeling better. He has been telling a joke to anyone who will listen. "A man took his wife around the world. When they got home, he asked her where she wanted to go for dinner. She said, 'Take me some place

I've never been.' He picked her up in his arms and carried her into the kitchen!"

Last time Pete said our World Cruise was a once-in-a-wife-time experience. Now I know he did not mean that. We won't go again for a year or two, but we are sure we will go again sometime. Holland America has been wonderful to us. We are spoiled with the level of service they have provided. Cruising has become part of our bones.

WORLD CRUISE RECIPES

Cooking classes are one of the features of a Holland America cruise. On this trip, Bernie Ruis, was Executive Chef de Cuisine. His food made the trip memorable.

JUMBO SHRIMP IN ALMOND SAUCE

Shell one pound of raw jumbo shrimp. Combine the shells with 2 ½ cups of water and 3 thin slices of fresh ginger. Simmer, uncovered, for 15 minutes, until the water reduces by half. Strain the liquid and reserve. Discard the shells.

Devein the shrimp, place in a bowl, season with 2 teaspoons curry powder, 2 cloves of crushed garlic and salt and pepper. Set aside. Heat 1 tablespoon mustard oil and 1 tablespoon vegetable oil (or use 2 tablespoons vegetable oil) in a large frying pan. Add to the oil 1 onion, sliced, ½ sliced seeded red bell pepper, ½ sliced green bell pepper, and 1 chayote or other mild flavored squash, peeled, pitted and cut into strips. Stir-fry for 5 minutes. Season with salt and pepper and keep warm.

Wipe out frying pan, add 1 tablespoon of butter and sauté shrimp for 5 minutes, until pink. Spoon over bed of vegetables and keep warm. Add 4 tablespoons of ground almonds (ground in a food processor) and 1 minced green chili pepper to pan, stir-fry for a few seconds, add the reserved shrimp stock and bring to a boil. Reduce the heat, stir in 3 tablespoons of light cream and simmer but do not boil for a few minutes. Pour sauce over the shrimp and vegetables and serve. Serves 3-4.

SAUTEED SHRIMP WITH CHILES

From Thailand comes this recipe for shrimp. The coconut cream, coconut milk and chili are typical of Thai cooking.

Peel ¾ pound of large shrimp and clean them. Sauté the shrimp with a little minced garlic for 2 to 3 minutes, until they are bright pink.

In a saucepan, heat ½ cup of coconut cream and add 2 tablespoons of red curry paste*, heating until fragrant. Bring 2 ½ cups of coconut milk to a boil and add the shrimp. Simmer until the shrimp are cooked—a few more minutes. Add 3 tablespoons fish sauce and 2 tablespoons of brown sugar, to taste. Place the shrimp and the coconut gravy on a serving platter and garnish with shreds of kaffir lime leaves, basil or cilantro leaves and 3 red chiles, cut into fine strips. If this dish is too hot, cool it by adding lime juice. Serves 3.

* Thai red and green curry paste are now available in our supermarkets, as are canned coconut milk and coconut cream.

MANGO BEEF

Harold, the chef in the Odyssey Restaurant, prepared this for us one day at cooking class. It was a hit.

Marinate together for two hours, ¾ lb. beef sirloin, cut into ½ inch cubes, 1 teaspoon cornstarch and 1 tablespoon oyster sauce. Peel a ripe mango and cut the flesh from the seed. Cut into ¾ inch cubes. Peel and core a large Granny Smith apple and cut into ½ inch cubes. Place a wok over high heat. Add 1 ½ tablespoons oil. Add 1 teaspoon minced ginger and cook, stirring, until fragrant. Add beef and stir-fry until no longer pink—1 ½ to 2 minutes. Remove meat and ginger from pan. Add another ½ tablespoon oil to wok. Add mango, apple and ¼ cup diced red bell pepper. Stir-fry for 2 minutes. Return meat to wok, add 2 tablespoons plum sauce, 1 tablespoon Chinese rice wine vinegar, 2 teaspoons soy sauce, ¼ cup whole macadamia nuts and ½ fresh red or green jalapeno chile, sliced. If needed, add a little more oyster sauce for flavor or some cornstarch if it needs thickening. Serves 3-4.

CREMÉ BRULEÉ

One of the reasons we travel is to eat things we never fix at home. This delicious dessert is well-loved and if you are thin enough, eat it as often as you like.

Mix together 12 egg yolks and ¾ cup of sugar. Beat on high speed for three minutes. Bring 2 cups of whole milk and 2 cups of heavy cream to a simmer. Add slowly to the egg and sugar mixture and stir. Pass through a sieve. Fill small pots with the mix, place in a pan with hot water halfway up the side and bake at 375° for 45 minutes. Cool out of the hot water and then chill. Once they are cold, sprinkle with brown sugar and then caramelize under a hot broiler for a minute or two. Serve immediately. The sugar crust will soften if the pots stand before serving. Serves 6.

HOLLAND AMERICA BREAD PUDDING

This famous dessert is served at noon in the Lido. Don't look for it in the Dining Room, for it is never served there. Besides, you need to help yourself to the vanilla sauce that accompanies it. Otherwise you may not get enough.

Combine 1 cup of milk and 1 cup of heavy cream and bring to a simmer, along with salt to taste, and 6 tablespoons of butter. If you have fresh vanilla beans, slit open three of them and add them to the simmering milk mixture. If not, add 2 teaspoons pure vanilla extract. Mix 5 eggs and ½ cup of sugar together and add the hot milk mixture to them, stirring. Strain it.

Arrange 1 loaf of sliced white bread with crusts cut off in a buttered baking pan in several layers. Put 1 oz. of raisins to soften in hot water for a few minutes. Drain and add them to the bread layers and cover with the milk mixture. Place the pan in a roasting pan filled ½ full with hot water. Bake at 350 for 40-50 minutes, until golden brown. Sprinkle with cinnamon sugar made of 1 teaspoon of cinnamon and 1 tablespoon sugar. Serve with Vanilla Sauce.

VANILLA SAUCE

Heat 1 ¾ cups milk to a boil. Place 4 egg yolks in a mixer bowl. Gradually add ½ cup of sugar, beating until the yolks are pale yellow. Pour the hot milk into the egg-sugar mixture in little drops, to warm the yolks gradually. Put in a saucepan, set over moderate heat, and stir slowly and carefully until the sauce thickens slightly. If you have a thermometer, heat to 165°. Do not let it simmer or the eggs will cook and separate. Beat off the heat for two minutes to cool it. Strain the mixture and cool it. Flavor with the seeds of 1 vanilla bean or 1 tablespoon of vanilla extract. Chill it.

CHOCOLATE TRUFFLES

Every formal night a candy dish of rich handmade chocolates and tiny cookies is brought to the dinner table at the end of the meal. These wonderful truffles are popular.

Bring 2 cups of whole milk and two cups of heavy cream to a simmer. Pour over two lbs. of good quality dark chocolate, finely chopped. Mix well and add 1 cup of unsalted butter that has been softened. Set aside to cool. With a spoon, form the chocolate into small balls, and place them so they do not touch each other on waxed paper. Leave to set for 12 hours in a cool place. Dust the balls with ground chocolate, cocoa or nuts. Store in the refrigerator. Makes 12-24 truffles.

MANGO PIE

This delicious dessert for a tropical dinner comes from Emerson House in Zanzibar, Tanzania.

Slice three or four ripe mangos into a buttered dish. Squeeze lemon juice over them. Top with a crumble topping made with 1 cup nuts, 1 cup flour, ½ cup butter, ½ cup brown sugar and 2 teaspoons cinnamon. Blend these ingredients in a food processor and sprinkle over the mangos. Bake at 350° until it begins to brown. Serves 4.

ZANZIBAR SPICE CAKE

This recipe includes some of the exports for which Zanzibar is famous. If you don't have ground cloves, grind whole cloves and a whole nutmeg in your coffee grinder. The flavor will be fresher. Perhaps a whole teaspoon of cloves is too much for some appetites. Try it and see.

Cream together ½ cup of butter and 1 ½ cups of sugar. Separate 4 eggs and set the whites aside. Add 4 egg yolks and mix in to the butter-sugar mixture. Add 2/3 cup of grated or ground semisweet chocolate.

Sift together 3 cups of flour, 1 teaspoon baking powder, 1 teaspoon cinnamon, a teaspoon ground cloves, and ½ teaspoon nutmeg. Alternate adding the dry ingredients and 1 cup of milk blended with 1 teaspoon of vanilla to the first mixture. Beat the four egg whites stiff. Stir one third of the egg whites into the batter to lighten it. Add the other egg whites, folding carefully. Bake in a greased tube pan for 55-60 minutes with the oven at 350°. Serves 12.

SEAFOAM FROSTING

Blend 2 egg whites, 1 ½ cups of brown sugar, 6 tablespoons of water, 2 teaspoons of light corn syrup and 1 teaspoon vanilla. Beat the mixture in the top of a double boiler, over simmering water, with a hand-held electric mixer for seven minutes. When cool, spread on the cooled spice cake.

COSTA RICAN ICED COFFEE

This idea comes from the Café′ Britt farm in Costa Rica. They serve this delicious drink in the late morning, but I think it would make a terrific summer dessert.

Grind Café Britt coffee beans and brew a pot of strong coffee. Cool it. Pour the coffee over ice cubes in tall glasses. Add sugar syrup to taste. Add a jigger of Kahlua, Amaretto, Gran Marnier or Tia Maria to the coffee. Float heavy cream on the top by pouring it into a spoon held level with the top surface of the coffee and letting it float over the surface. Sprinkle with a little cinnamon. Note: to make sugar syrup, boil equal amounts of sugar and water for five minutes. Serves 4.

ORDER FORM

Send postal orders to *Warthog Press*, Box 241, 435 Main Street, Dunkirk, NY 14048

Title: ***Around the World by Cruise Ship—People, Places, Politics***

Name:

Address:

City: State Zip:

Telephone: email address:

Autographed?

Dedicated to whom:

Include your check for $16 for the book
plus $2 for shipping and handling ($18 total).